Disclaimer

The publisher of this book is by no way associated with the National Institute of Standards and Technology (NIST). The NIST did not publish this book. It was published by 50 page publications under the public domain license.

50 Page Publications.

Book Title: Recommendation for Block Cipher Modes of Operation Methods and Techniques

Book Author: Morris J. Dworkin;

Book Abstract: This recommendation defines five confidentiality modes of operation for use with an underlying symmetric key block cipher algorithm: Electronic Codebook (ECB), Cipher Block Chaining (CBC), Cipher Feedback (CFB), Output Feedback (OFB), and Counter (CTR). Used with an underlying block cipher algorithm that is approved in a Federal Information Processing Standard (FIPS), these modes can provide cryptographic protection for sensitive, but unclassified, computer data.

Citation: NIST SP - 800-38A

Keyword: Computer security; cryptography; data security; block cipher; encryption; Federal Information Processing Standard; mode of operation.

NIST Special Publication 800-38A
2001 Edition

Recommendation for Block Cipher Modes of Operation

Methods and Techniques

NIST

**National Institute of
Standards and Technology**
Technology Administration
U.S. Department of Commerce

Morris Dworkin

C O M P U T E R   S E C U R I T Y

COMPUTER SECURITY

Computer Security Division
Information Technology Laboratory
National Institute of Standards and Technology
Gaithersburg, MD 20899-8930

December 2001

U.S. Department of Commerce
Donald L. Evans, Secretary

Technology Administration
Phillip J. Bond, Under Secretary of Commerce for Technology

National Institute of Standards and Technology
Arden L. Bement, Jr., Director

Reports on Information Security Technology

The Information Technology Laboratory (ITL) at the National Institute of Standards and Technology (NIST) promotes the U.S. economy and public welfare by providing technical leadership for the Nation's measurement and standards infrastructure. ITL develops tests, test methods, reference data, proof of concept implementations, and technical analyses to advance the development and productive use of information technology. ITL's responsibilities include the development of technical, physical, administrative, and management standards and guidelines for the cost-effective security and privacy of sensitive unclassified information in Federal computer systems. This Special Publication 800-series reports on ITL's research, guidance, and outreach efforts in computer security, and its collaborative activities with industry, government, and academic organizations.

National Institute of Standards and Technology Special Publication 800-38A 2001 ED
Natl. Inst. Stand. Technol. Spec. Publ. 800-38A 2001 ED, 66 pages (December 2001)
CODEN: NSPUE2

U.S. GOVERNMENT PRINTING OFFICE
WASHINGTON: 2001

For sale by the Superintendent of Documents, U.S. Government Printing Office
Internet: bookstore.gpo.gov — Phone: (202) 512-1800 — Fax: (202) 512-2250
Mail: Stop SSOP, Washington, DC 20402-0001

Abstract

This recommendation defines five confidentiality modes of operation for use with an underlying symmetric key block cipher algorithm: Electronic Codebook (ECB), Cipher Block Chaining (CBC), Cipher Feedback (CFB), Output Feedback (OFB), and Counter (CTR). Used with an underlying block cipher algorithm that is approved in a Federal Information Processing Standard (FIPS), these modes can provide cryptographic protection for sensitive, but unclassified, computer data.

KEY WORDS: Computer security; cryptography; data security; block cipher; encryption; Federal Information Processing Standard; mode of operation.

Table of Contents

Table of Figures

1 Purpose

This publication provides recommendations regarding modes of operation to be used with symmetric key block cipher algorithms.

2 Authority

This document has been developed by the National Institute of Standards and Technology (NIST) in furtherance of its statutory responsibilities under the Computer Security Act of 1987 (Public Law 100-235) and the Information Technology Management Reform Act of 1996, specifically 15 U.S.C. 278 g-3(a)(5). This is not a guideline within the meaning of 15 U.S.C. 278 g-3 (a)(5).

This recommendation is neither a standard nor a guideline, and as such, is neither mandatory nor binding on Federal agencies. Federal agencies and non-government organizations may use this recommendation on a voluntary basis. It is not subject to copyright.

Nothing in this recommendation should be taken to contradict standards and guidelines that have been made mandatory and binding upon Federal agencies by the Secretary of Commerce under his statutory authority. Nor should this recommendation be interpreted as altering or superseding the existing authorities of the Secretary of Commerce, the Director of the Office of Management and Budget, or any other Federal official.

Conformance testing for implementations of the modes of operation that are specified in this recommendation will be conducted within the framework of the Cryptographic Module Validation Program (CMVP), a joint effort of the NIST and the Communications Security Establishment of the Government of Canada. An implementation of a mode of operation must adhere to the requirements in this recommendation in order to be validated under the CMVP.

3 Introduction

This recommendation specifies five confidentiality modes of operation for symmetric key block cipher algorithms, such as the algorithm specified in FIPS Pub. 197, the Advanced Encryption Standard (AES) [2]. The modes may be used in conjunction with any symmetric key block cipher algorithm that is approved by a Federal Information Processing Standard (FIPS). The five modes—the Electronic Codebook (ECB), Cipher Block Chaining (CBC), Cipher Feedback (CFB), Output Feedback (OFB), and Counter (CTR) modes—can provide data confidentiality.

Two FIPS publications already approve confidentiality modes of operation for two particular block cipher algorithms. FIPS Pub. 81 [4] specifies the ECB, CBC, CFB, and OFB modes of the Data Encryption Standard (DES). FIPS Pub. 46-3 [3] approves the seven modes that are specified in ANSI X9.52 [1]. Four of these modes are equivalent to the ECB, CBC, CFB, and OFB modes with the Triple DES algorithm (TDEA) as the underlying block cipher; the other three modes in ANSI X9.52 are variants of the CBC, CFB, and OFB modes of Triple DES that use interleaving or pipelining.

Thus, there are three new elements in this recommendation: 1) the extension of the four confidentiality modes in FIPS Pub 81 for use with any FIPS-approved block cipher; 2) the revision of the requirements for these modes; and 3) the specification of an additional confidentiality mode, the CTR mode, for use with any FIPS-approved block cipher.

4 Definitions, Abbreviations, and Symbols

4.1 Definitions and Abbreviations

Bit	A binary digit: 0 or 1.
Bit Error	The substitution of a '0' bit for a '1' bit, or vice versa.
Bit String	An ordered sequence of 0's and 1's.
Block Cipher	A family of functions and their inverse functions that is parameterized by cryptographic keys; the functions map bit strings of a fixed length to bit strings of the same length.
Block Size	The number of bits in an input (or output) block of the block cipher.
CBC	Cipher Block Chaining.
CFB	Cipher Feedback.
Ciphertext	Encrypted data.
Confidentiality Mode	A mode that is used to encipher plaintext and decipher ciphertext. The confidentiality modes in this recommendation are the ECB, CBC, CFB, OFB, and CTR modes.
CTR	Counter.
Cryptographic Key	A parameter used in the block cipher algorithm that determines the forward cipher operation and the inverse cipher operation.
Data Block (Block)	A sequence of bits whose length is the block size of the block cipher.
Data Segment (Segment)	In the CFB mode, a sequence of bits whose length is a parameter that does not exceed the block size.
Decryption (Deciphering)	The process of a confidentiality mode that transforms encrypted data into the original usable data.
ECB	Electronic Codebook.
Encryption (Enciphering)	The process of a confidentiality mode that transforms usable data into an unreadable form.

Exclusive-OR	The bitwise addition, modulo 2, of two bit strings of equal length.
FIPS	Federal Information Processing Standard.
Forward Cipher Function (Forward Cipher Operation)	One of the two functions of the block cipher algorithm that is selected by the cryptographic key.
Initialization Vector (IV)	A data block that some modes of operation require as an additional initial input.
Input Block	A data block that is an input to either the forward cipher function or the inverse cipher function of the block cipher algorithm.
Inverse Cipher Function (Inverse Cipher Operation)	The function that reverses the transformation of the forward cipher function when the same cryptographic key is used.
Least Significant Bit(s)	The right-most bit(s) of a bit string.
Mode of Operation (Mode)	An algorithm for the cryptographic transformation of data that features a symmetric key block cipher algorithm.
Most Significant Bit(s)	The left-most bit(s) of a bit string.
Nonce	A value that is used only once.
Octet	A group of eight binary digits.
OFB	Output Feedback.
Output Block	A data block that is an output of either the forward cipher function or the inverse cipher function of the block cipher algorithm.
Plaintext	Usable data that is formatted as input to a mode.

4.2 Symbols

4.2.1 Variables

b	The block size, in bits.
j	The index to a sequence of data blocks or data segments ordered from left to right.
n	The number of data blocks or data segments in the plaintext.
s	The number of bits in a data segment.
u	The number of bits in the last plaintext or ciphertext block.
C_j	The jth ciphertext block.
$C_j^{\#}$	The jth ciphertext segment.
C_n^{*}	The last block of the ciphertext, which may be a partial block.
I_j	The jth input block.
IV	The initialization vector.
K	The secret key.
O_j	The jth output block.
P_j	The jth plaintext block.
$P_j^{\#}$	The jth plaintext segment.
P_n^{*}	The last block of the plaintext, which may be a partial block.
T_j	The jth counter block.

4.2.2 Operations and Functions

$X \mid Y$	The concatenation of two bit strings X and Y.
$X \oplus Y$	The bitwise exclusive-OR of two bit strings X and Y of the same length.
$CIPH_K(X)$	The forward cipher function of the block cipher algorithm under the key K applied to the data block X.

$CIPH^{-1}{}_{K}(X)$ The inverse cipher function of the block cipher algorithm under the key K applied to the data block X.

$LSB_m(X)$ The bit string consisting of the m least significant bits of the bit string X.

$MSB_m(X)$ The bit string consisting of the m most significant bits of the bit string X.

$[x]_m$ The binary representation of the non-negative integer x, in m bits, where $x < 2^m$.

5 Preliminaries

5.1 Underlying Block Cipher Algorithm

This recommendation assumes that a FIPS-approved symmetric key block cipher algorithm has been chosen as the underlying algorithm, and that a secret, random key, denoted K, has been established among all of the parties to the communication. The cryptographic key regulates the functioning of the block cipher algorithm and, thus, by extension, regulates the functioning of the mode. The specifications of the block cipher and algorithms and the modes are public, so the security of the mode depends, at a minimum, on the secrecy of the key.

A confidentiality mode of operation of the block cipher algorithm consists of two processes that are inverses of each other: encryption and decryption. Encryption is the transformation of a usable message, called the plaintext, into an unreadable form, called the ciphertext; decryption is the transformation that recovers the plaintext from the ciphertext.

For any given key, the underlying block cipher algorithm of the mode also consists of two functions that are inverses of each other. These two functions are often called encryption and decryption, but in this recommendation, those terms are reserved for the processes of the confidentiality modes. Instead, as part of the choice of the block cipher algorithm, one of the two functions is designated as the forward cipher function, denoted $CIPH_K$; the other function is then called the inverse cipher function, denoted $CIPH^{-1}_K$. The inputs and outputs of both functions are called input blocks and output blocks. The input and output blocks of the block cipher algorithm have the same bit length, called the block size, denoted b.

5.2 Representation of the Plaintext and the Ciphertext

For all of the modes in this recommendation, the plaintext must be represented as a sequence of bit strings; the requirements on the lengths of the bit strings vary according to the mode:

For the ECB and CBC modes, the total number of bits in the plaintext must be a multiple of the block size, b; in other words, for some positive integer n, the total number of bits in the plaintext must be nb. The plaintext consists of a sequence of n bit strings, each with bit length b. The bit strings in the sequence are called data blocks, and the plaintext is denoted $P_1, P_2, ..., P_n$.

For the CFB mode, the total number of bits in the plaintext must be a multiple of a parameter, denoted s, that does not exceed the block size; in other words, for some positive integer n, the total number of bits in the message must be ns. The plaintext consists of a sequence of n bit strings, each with bit length s. The bit strings in the sequence are called data segments, and the plaintext is denoted $P^\#_1, P^\#_2, ..., P^\#_n$.

For the OFB and CTR modes, the plaintext need not be a multiple of the block size. Let n and u denote the unique pair of positive integers such that the total number of bits in the message is $(n-1)b+u$, where $1 \le u \le b$. The plaintext consists of a sequence of n bit strings, in which the bit length of the last bit string is u, and the bit length of the other bit strings is b. The sequence is denoted $P_1, P_2, ..., P_{n-1}, P^*_n$, and the bit strings are called data blocks, although the last bit string,

P^*_n , may not be a complete block.

For each mode, the encryption process transforms every plaintext data block or segment into a corresponding ciphertext data block or segment with the same bit length, so that the ciphertext is a sequence of data blocks or segments. The ciphertext is denoted as follows: for the ECB and CBC modes, C_1, C_2,..., C_n; for the CFB mode, $C^\#_1$, $C^\#_2$,..., $C^\#_n$; and, for the OFB and CTR modes, C_1, C_2,..., C_{n-1}, C^*_n, where C^*_n may be a partial block.

The formatting of the plaintext, including in some cases the appending of padding bits to form complete data blocks or data segments, is outside the scope of this recommendation. Padding is discussed in Appendix A.

5.3 Initialization Vectors

The input to the encryption processes of the CBC, CFB, and OFB modes includes, in addition to the plaintext, a data block called the initialization vector (IV), denoted IV. The IV is used in an initial step in the encryption of a message and in the corresponding decryption of the message.

The IV need not be secret; however, for the CBC and CFB modes, the IV for any particular execution of the encryption process must be unpredictable, and, for the OFB mode, unique IVs must be used for each execution of the encryption process. The generation of IVs is discussed in Appendix C.

5.4 Examples of Operations and Functions

The concatenation operation on bit strings is denoted | ; for example, 001 | 10111 = 00110111.

Given bit strings of equal length, the exclusive-OR operation, denoted $\oplus$, specifies the addition, modulo 2, of the bits in each bit position, i.e., without carries. Thus, 10011 $\oplus$ 10101= 00110, for example.

The functions LSB_s and MSB_s return the s least significant bits and the s most significant bits of their arguments. For example, $LSB_3(111011010) = 010$, and $MSB_4(111011010) = 1110$.

Given a positive integer m and a non-negative (decimal) integer x that is less than 2^m, the binary representation of x in m bits is denoted $[x]_m$. For example, $[45]_8 = 00101101$.

8

6 Block Cipher Modes of Operation

The mathematical specifications of the five modes are given in Sections 6.1-6.5, along with descriptions, illustrations, and comments on the potential for parallel processing.

6.1 The Electronic Codebook Mode

The Electronic Codebook (ECB) mode is a confidentiality mode that features, for a given key, the assignment of a fixed ciphertext block to each plaintext block, analogous to the assignment of code words in a codebook. The Electronic Codebook (ECB) mode is defined as follows:

$$\text{ECB Encryption:} \qquad C_j = CIPH_K(P_j) \qquad\qquad \text{for } j = 1 \ldots n.$$

$$\text{ECB Decryption:} \qquad P_j = CIPH^{-1}{}_K(C_j) \qquad\qquad \text{for } j = 1 \ldots n.$$

In ECB encryption, the forward cipher function is applied directly and independently to each block of the plaintext. The resulting sequence of output blocks is the ciphertext.

In ECB decryption, the inverse cipher function is applied directly and independently to each block of the ciphertext. The resulting sequence of output blocks is the plaintext.

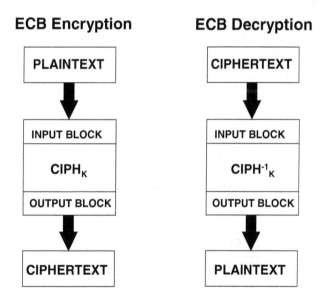

Figure 1: The ECB Mode

In ECB encryption and ECB decryption, multiple forward cipher functions and inverse cipher functions can be computed in parallel.

In the ECB mode, under a given key, any given plaintext block always gets encrypted to the same ciphertext block. If this property is undesirable in a particular application, the ECB mode should not be used.

The ECB mode is illustrated in Figure 1.

6.2 The Cipher Block Chaining Mode

The Cipher Block Chaining (CBC) mode is a confidentiality mode whose encryption process features the combining ("chaining") of the plaintext blocks with the previous ciphertext blocks. The CBC mode requires an IV to combine with the first plaintext block. The IV need not be secret, but it must be unpredictable; the generation of such IVs is discussed in Appendix C. Also, the integrity of the IV should be protected, as discussed in Appendix D. The CBC mode is defined as follows:

CBC Encryption:
$$C_1 = CIPH_K(P_1 \oplus IV);$$
$$C_j = CIPH_K(P_j \oplus C_{j-1}) \qquad \text{for } j = 2 \dots n.$$

CBC Decryption:
$$P_1 = CIPH^{-1}_K(C_1) \oplus IV;$$
$$P_j = CIPH^{-1}_K(C_j) \oplus C_{j-1} \qquad \text{for } j = 2 \dots n.$$

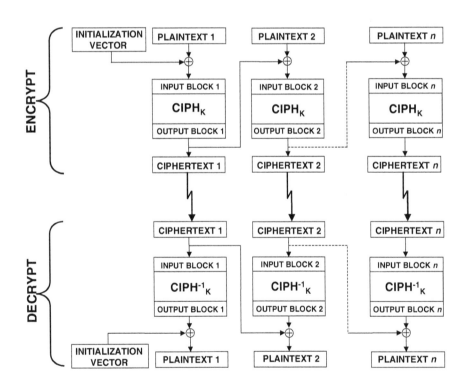

Figure 2: The CBC Mode

In CBC encryption, the first input block is formed by exclusive-ORing the first block of the plaintext with the IV. The forward cipher function is applied to the first input block, and the resulting output block is the first block of the ciphertext. This output block is also exclusive-ORed with the second plaintext data block to produce the second input block, and the forward cipher function is applied to produce the second output block. This output block, which is the second ciphertext block, is exclusive-ORed with the next plaintext block to form the next input block. Each successive plaintext block is exclusive-ORed with the previous output/ciphertext block to produce the new input block. The forward cipher function is applied to each input block to produce the ciphertext block.

In CBC decryption, the inverse cipher function is applied to the first ciphertext block, and the resulting output block is exclusive-ORed with the initialization vector to recover the first plaintext block. The inverse cipher function is also applied to the second ciphertext block, and the resulting output block is exclusive-ORed with the first ciphertext block to recover the second plaintext block. In general, to recover any plaintext block (except the first), the inverse cipher function is applied to the corresponding ciphertext block, and the resulting block is exclusive-ORed with the previous ciphertext block.

In CBC encryption, the input block to each forward cipher operation (except the first) depends on the result of the previous forward cipher operation, so the forward cipher operations cannot be performed in parallel. In CBC decryption, however, the input blocks for the inverse cipher function, i.e., the ciphertext blocks, are immediately available, so that multiple inverse cipher operations can be performed in parallel.

The CBC mode is illustrated in Figure 2.

6.3 The Cipher Feedback Mode

The Cipher Feedback (CFB) mode is a confidentiality mode that features the feedback of successive ciphertext segments into the input blocks of the forward cipher to generate output blocks that are exclusive-ORed with the plaintext to produce the ciphertext, and vice versa. The CFB mode requires an IV as the initial input block. The IV need not be secret, but it must be unpredictable; the generation of such IVs is discussed in Appendix C.

The CFB mode also requires an integer parameter, denoted s, such that $1 \leq s \leq b$. In the specification of the CFB mode below, each plaintext segment ($P^{\#}_j$) and ciphertext segment ($C^{\#}_j$) consists of s bits. The value of s is sometimes incorporated into the name of the mode, e.g., the 1-bit CFB mode, the 8-bit CFB mode, the 64-bit CFB mode, or the 128-bit CFB mode.

The CFB mode is defined as follows:

CFB Encryption: $I_1 = IV;$

$I_j = LSB_{b-s}(I_{j-1}) \mid C^{\#}_{j-1}$ for $j = 2 \dots n;$

$O_j = CIPH_K(I_j)$ for $j = 1, 2 \dots n;$

$C^{\#}_j = P^{\#}_j \oplus MSB_s(O_j)$ for $j = 1, 2 \dots n.$

CFB Decryption: $I_1 = IV;$

$I_j = LSB_{b-s}(I_{j-1}) \mid C^{\#}_{j-1}$ for $j = 2 \dots n;$

$$O_j = CIPH_K(I_j) \qquad\qquad \text{for } j = 1, 2 \ldots n;$$
$$P^\#_j = C^\#_j \oplus MSB_s(O_j) \qquad\qquad \text{for } j = 1, 2 \ldots n.$$

In CFB encryption, the first input block is the IV, and the forward cipher operation is applied to the IV to produce the first output block. The first ciphertext segment is produced by exclusive-ORing the first plaintext segment with the *s* most significant bits of the first output block. (The remaining *b-s* bits of the first output block are discarded.) The *b-s* least significant bits of the IV are then concatenated with the *s* bits of the first ciphertext segment to form the second input block. An alternative description of the formation of the second input block is that the bits of the first input block circularly shift *s* positions to the left, and then the ciphertext segment replaces the *s* least significant bits of the result.

The process is repeated with the successive input blocks until a ciphertext segment is produced from every plaintext segment. In general, each successive input block is enciphered to produce an output block. The *s* most significant bits of each output block are exclusive-ORed with the corresponding plaintext segment to form a ciphertext segment. Each ciphertext segment (except the last one) is "fed back" into the previous input block, as described above, to form a new input block. The feedback can be described in terms of the individual bits in the strings as follows: if $i_1 i_2 \ldots i_b$ is the *j*th input block, and $c_1 c_2 \ldots c_s$ is the *j*th ciphertext segment, then the $(j+1)^{\text{th}}$ input block is $i_{s+1} i_{s+2} \ldots i_b\, c_1 c_2 \ldots c_s$.

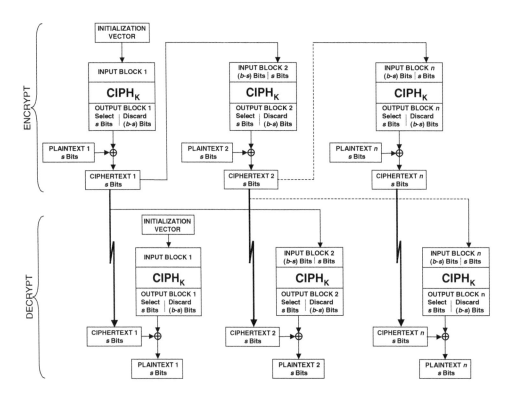

Figure 3: The CFB Mode

In CFB decryption, the IV is the first input block, and each successive input block is formed as in CFB encryption, by concatenating the *b-s* least significant bits of the previous input block with

12

the *s* most significant bits of the previous ciphertext. The *forward cipher* function is applied to each input block to produce the output blocks. The *s* most significant bits of the output blocks are exclusive-ORed with the corresponding ciphertext segments to recover the plaintext segments.

In CFB encryption, like CBC encryption, the input block to each forward cipher function (except the first) depends on the result of the previous forward cipher function; therefore, multiple forward cipher operations cannot be performed in parallel. In CFB decryption, the required forward cipher operations can be performed in parallel if the input blocks are first constructed (in series) from the IV and the ciphertext.

The CFB mode is illustrated in Figure 3.

6.4 The Output Feedback Mode

The Output Feedback (OFB) mode is a confidentiality mode that features the iteration of the forward cipher on an IV to generate a sequence of output blocks that are exclusive-ORed with the plaintext to produce the ciphertext, and vice versa. The OFB mode requires that the IV is a nonce, i.e., the IV must be unique for each execution of the mode under the given key; the generation of such IVs is discussed in Appendix C. The OFB mode is defined as follows:

OFB Encryption:

$$I_1 = IV;$$
$$I_j = O_{j-1} \qquad \text{for } j = 2 \ldots n;$$
$$O_j = CIPH_K(I_j) \qquad \text{for } j = 1, 2 \ldots n;$$
$$C_j = P_j \oplus O_j \qquad \text{for } j = 1, 2 \ldots n\text{-}1;$$
$$C^*_n = P^*_n \oplus MSB_u(O_n).$$

OFB Decryption:

$$I_1 = IV;$$
$$I_j = O_{j-1} \qquad \text{for } j = 2 \ldots n;$$
$$O_j = CIPH_K(I_j) \qquad \text{for } j = 1, 2 \ldots n;$$
$$P_j = C_j \oplus O_j \qquad \text{for } j = 1, 2 \ldots n\text{-}1;$$
$$P^*_n = C^*_n \oplus MSB_u(O_n).$$

In OFB encryption, the IV is transformed by the forward cipher function to produce the first output block. The first output block is exclusive-ORed with the first plaintext block to produce the first ciphertext block. The forward cipher function is then invoked on the first output block to produce the second output block. The second output block is exclusive-ORed with the second plaintext block to produce the second ciphertext block, and the forward cipher function is invoked on the second output block to produce the third output block. Thus, the successive output blocks are produced from applying the forward cipher function to the previous output blocks, and the output blocks are exclusive-ORed with the corresponding plaintext blocks to produce the ciphertext blocks. For the last block, which may be a partial block of *u* bits, the most significant *u* bits of the last output block are used for the exclusive-OR operation; the remaining *b-u* bits of the last output block are discarded.

In OFB decryption, the IV is transformed by the *forward cipher* function to produce the first output block. The first output block is exclusive-ORed with the first ciphertext block to recover the first plaintext block. The first output block is then transformed by the forward cipher function to produce the second output block. The second output block is exclusive-ORed with the second ciphertext block to produce the second plaintext block, and the second output block is also transformed by the forward cipher function to produce the third output block. Thus, the successive output blocks are produced from applying the forward cipher function to the previous output blocks, and the output blocks are exclusive-ORed with the corresponding ciphertext blocks to recover the plaintext blocks. For the last block, which may be a partial block of u bits, the most significant u bits of the last output block are used for the exclusive-OR operation; the remaining b-u bits of the last output block are discarded.

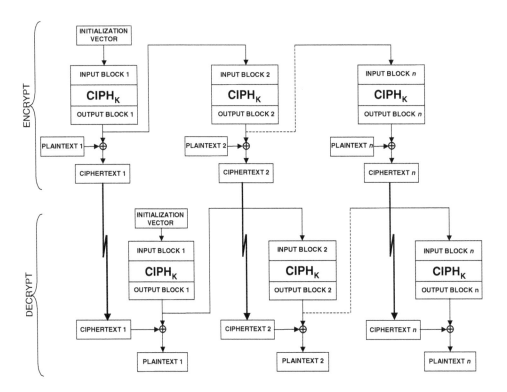

Figure 4: The OFB Mode

In both OFB encryption and OFB decryption, each forward cipher function (except the first) depends on the results of the previous forward cipher function; therefore, multiple forward cipher functions cannot be performed in parallel. However, if the IV is known, the output blocks can be generated prior to the availability of the plaintext or ciphertext data.

The OFB mode requires a unique IV for every message that is ever encrypted under the given key. If, contrary to this requirement, the same IV is used for the encryption of more than one message, then the confidentiality of those messages may be compromised. In particular, if a plaintext block of any of these messages is known, say, the jth plaintext block, then the jth output of the forward cipher function can be determined easily from the jth ciphertext block of the message. This information allows the jth plaintext block of any other message that is encrypted

14

using the same IV to be easily recovered from the jth ciphertext block of that message.

Confidentiality may similarly be compromised if *any* of the input blocks to the forward cipher function for the encryption of a message is designated as the IV for the encryption of another message under the given key.

The OFB mode is illustrated in Figure 4.

6.5 The Counter Mode

The Counter (CTR) mode is a confidentiality mode that features the application of the forward cipher to a set of input blocks, called counters, to produce a sequence of output blocks that are exclusive-ORed with the plaintext to produce the ciphertext, and vice versa. The sequence of counters must have the property that each block in the sequence is different from every other block. This condition is not restricted to a single message: across all of the messages that are encrypted under the given key, all of the counters must be distinct. In this recommendation, the counters for a given message are denoted T_1, T_2, ... , T_n. Methods for generating counters are discussed in Appendix B. Given a sequence of counters, T_1 , T_2 , ... , T_n, the CTR mode is defined as follows:

CTR Encryption: $O_j = CIPH_K(T_j)$ for $j = 1, 2 ... n$;
 $C_j = P_j \oplus O_j$ for $j = 1, 2 ... n\text{-}1$;
 $C^*_n = P^*_n \oplus MSB_u(O_n)$.

CTR Decryption: $O_j = CIPH_K(T_j)$ for $j = 1, 2 ... n$;
 $P_j = C_j \oplus O_j$ for $j = 1, 2 ... n\text{-}1$;
 $P^*_n = C^*_n \oplus MSB_u(O_n)$.

In CTR encryption, the forward cipher function is invoked on each counter block, and the resulting output blocks are exclusive-ORed with the corresponding plaintext blocks to produce the ciphertext blocks. For the last block, which may be a partial block of u bits, the most significant u bits of the last output block are used for the exclusive-OR operation; the remaining b-u bits of the last output block are discarded.

In CTR decryption, the forward cipher function is invoked on each counter block, and the resulting output blocks are exclusive-ORed with the corresponding ciphertext blocks to recover the plaintext blocks. For the last block, which may be a partial block of u bits, the most significant u bits of the last output block are used for the exclusive-OR operation; the remaining b-u bits of the last output block are discarded.

In both CTR encryption and CTR decryption, the forward cipher functions can be performed in parallel; similarly, the plaintext block that corresponds to any particular ciphertext block can be recovered independently from the other plaintext blocks if the corresponding counter block can be determined. Moreover, the forward cipher functions can be applied to the counters prior to the availability of the plaintext or ciphertext data.

15

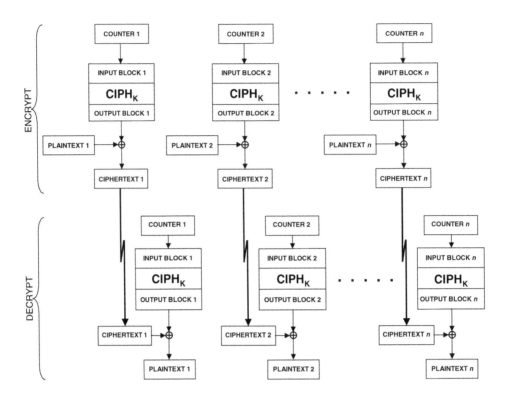

Figure 5: The CTR Mode

The CTR mode is illustrated in Figure 5.

Appendix A: Padding

For the ECB, CBC, and CFB modes, the plaintext must be a sequence of one or more complete data blocks (or, for CFB mode, data segments). In other words, for these three modes, the total number of bits in the plaintext must be a positive multiple of the block (or segment) size.

If the data string to be encrypted does not initially satisfy this property, then the formatting of the plaintext must entail an increase in the number of bits. A common way to achieve the necessary increase is to append some extra bits, called padding, to the trailing end of the data string as the last step in the formatting of the plaintext. An example of a padding method is to append a single '1' bit to the data string and then to pad the resulting string by as few '0' bits, possibly none, as are necessary to complete the final block (segment). Other methods may be used; in general, the formatting of the plaintext is outside the scope of this recommendation.

For the above padding method, the padding bits can be removed unambiguously, provided the receiver can determine that the message is indeed padded. One way to ensure that the receiver does not mistakenly remove bits from an unpadded message is to require the sender to pad every message, including messages in which the final block (segment) is already complete. For such messages, an entire block (segment) of padding is appended. Alternatively, such messages can be sent without padding if, for every message, the existence of padding can be reliably inferred, e.g., from a message length indicator.

Appendix B: Generation of Counter Blocks

The specification of the CTR mode requires a unique counter block for each plaintext block that is ever encrypted under a given key, across all messages. If, contrary to this requirement, a counter block is used repeatedly, then the confidentiality of all of the plaintext blocks corresponding to that counter block may be compromised. In particular, if any plaintext block that is encrypted using a given counter block is known, then the output of the forward cipher function can be determined easily from the associated ciphertext block. This output allows any other plaintext blocks that are encrypted using the same counter block to be easily recovered from their associated ciphertext blocks.

There are two aspects to satisfying the uniqueness requirement. First, an incrementing function for generating the counter blocks from any initial counter block can ensure that counter blocks do not repeat within a given message. Second, the initial counter blocks, T_1, must be chosen to ensure that counters are unique across all messages that are encrypted under the given key.

B.1   The Standard Incrementing Function

In general, given the initial counter block for a message, the successive counter blocks are derived by applying an incrementing function. As in the above specifications of the modes, n is the number of blocks in the given plaintext message, and b is the number of bits in the block.

The standard incrementing function can apply either to an entire block or to a part of a block. Let m be the number of bits in the specific part of the block to be incremented; thus, m is a positive integer such that $m \leq b$. Any string of m bits can be regarded as the binary representation of a non-negative integer x that is strictly less than 2^m. The standard incrementing function takes $[x]_m$ and returns $[x+1 \bmod 2^m]_m$.

For example, let the standard incrementing function apply to the five least significant bits of eight bit blocks, so that $b=8$ and $m=5$ (unrealistically small values); let * represent each unknown bit in this example, and let ***11110 represent a block to be incremented. The following sequence of blocks results from four applications of the standard incrementing function:

$$* * * 1\,1\,1\,1\,0$$
$$* * * 1\,1\,1\,1\,1$$
$$* * * 0\,0\,0\,0\,0$$
$$* * * 0\,0\,0\,0\,1$$
$$* * * 0\,0\,0\,1\,0.$$

Counter blocks in which a given set of m bits are incremented by the standard incrementing function satisfy the uniqueness requirement *within the given message* provided that $n \leq 2^m$. Whether the uniqueness requirement for counter blocks is satisfied across all messages that are encrypted under a given key then depends on the choices of the initial counter blocks for the messages, as discussed in the next section.

This recommendation permits the use of any other incrementing function that generates n unique strings of m bits in succession from the allowable initial strings. For example, if the initial string of m bits is not the "zero" string, i.e., if it contains at least one '1' bit, then an incrementing function can be constructed from a linear feedback shift register that is specialized to ensure a sufficiently large period; see Ref. [5] for information about linear feedback shift registers.

B.2 Choosing Initial Counter Blocks

The initial counter blocks, T_1, for each message that is encrypted under the given key must be chosen in a manner than ensures the uniqueness of all the counter blocks across all the messages. Two examples of approaches to choosing the initial counter blocks are given in this section.

In the first approach, for a given key, all plaintext messages are encrypted sequentially. Within the messages, the same fixed set of m bits of the counter block is incremented by the standard incrementing function. The initial counter block for the initial plaintext message may be any string of b bits. The initial counter block for any subsequent message can be obtained by applying the standard incrementing function to the fixed set of m bits of the final counter block of the previous message. In effect, all of the plaintext messages that are ever encrypted under the given key are concatenated into a single message; consequently, the total number of plaintext blocks must not exceed 2^m. Procedures should be established to ensure the maintenance of the state of the final counter block of the latest encrypted message, and to ensure the proper sequencing of the messages.

A second approach to satisfying the uniqueness property across messages is to assign to each message a unique string of $b/2$ bits (rounding up, if b is odd), in other words, a message nonce, and to incorporate the message nonce into every counter block for the message. The leading $b/2$ bits (rounding up, if b is odd) of each counter block would be the message nonce, and the standard incrementing function would be applied to the remaining m bits to provide an index to the counter blocks for the message. Thus, if N is the message nonce for a given message, then the jth counter block is given by $T_j = N \mid [j]_m$, for $j = 1...n$. The number of blocks, n, in any message must satisfy $n < 2^m$. A procedure should be established to ensure the uniqueness of the message nonces.

This recommendation allows other methods and approaches for achieving the uniqueness property. Validation that an implementation of the CTR mode conforms to this recommendation will typically include an examination of the procedures for assuring the uniqueness of counter blocks within messages and across all messages that are encrypted under a given key.

Appendix C: Generation of Initialization Vectors

The CBC, CFB, and OFB modes require an initialization vector as input, in addition to the plaintext. An IV must be generated for each execution of the encryption operation, and the same IV is necessary for the corresponding execution of the decryption operation. Therefore, the IV, or information that is sufficient to calculate the IV, must be available to each party to the communication.

The IV need not be secret, so the IV, or information sufficient to determine the IV, may be transmitted with the ciphertext.

For the CBC and CFB modes, the IVs must be unpredictable. In particular, for any given plaintext, it must not be possible to predict the IV that will be associated to the plaintext in advance of the generation of the IV.

There are two recommended methods for generating unpredictable IVs. The first method is to apply the forward cipher function, under the same key that is used for the encryption of the plaintext, to a nonce. The nonce must be a data block that is unique to each execution of the encryption operation. For example, the nonce may be a counter, as described in Appendix B, or a message number. The second method is to generate a random data block using a FIPS-approved random number generator.

For the OFB mode, the IV need not be unpredictable, but it must be a nonce that is unique to each execution of the encryption operation. For example, the nonce may be a counter, as described in Appendix B, or a message number.

If, contrary to this requirement, the same IV is used for the OFB encryption of more than one message, then the confidentiality of those messages may be compromised. In particular, if a plaintext block of any of these messages is known, say, the jth plaintext block, then the jth output of the forward cipher function can be determined easily from the jth ciphertext block of the message. This information allows the jth plaintext block of any other message that is encrypted using the same IV to be easily recovered from the jth ciphertext block of that message.

Confidentiality may similarly be compromised if *any* of the input blocks to the forward cipher function for the OFB encryption of a message is designated as the IV for the encryption of another message under the given key. One consequence of this observation is that IVs for the OFB mode should not be generated by invoking the block cipher on another IV.

Validation that an implementation of the CBC, CFB, or OFB mode conforms to this recommendation will typically include an examination of the procedures for assuring the unpredictability or uniqueness of the IV.

Appendix D: Error Properties

A bit error is the substitution of a '0' bit for a '1' bit, or vice versa. This appendix contains a discussion of the effects of bit errors in ciphertext blocks (or segments), counter blocks, and IVs on the modes in this recommendation. Insertion or deletion of bits into ciphertext blocks (or segments) is also discussed.

For any confidentiality mode, if there are any bit errors in a single ciphertext block (or segment), then the decryption of that ciphertext block (or segment) will be incorrect, i.e., it will differ from the original plaintext block (or segment). In the CFB, OFB, and CTR modes, the bit error(s) in the decrypted ciphertext block (or segment) occur in the same bit position(s) as in the ciphertext block (or segment); the other bit positions are not affected. In the ECB and CBC modes, a bit error may occur, independently, in any bit position of the decrypted ciphertext block, with an expected error rate of fifty percent, depending on the strength of the underlying block cipher.

For the ECB, OFB, and CTR modes, bit errors within a ciphertext block do not affect the decryption of any other blocks. In the CBC mode, any bit positions that contain bit errors in a ciphertext block will also contain bit errors in the decryption of the succeeding ciphertext block; the other bit positions are not affected. In the CFB mode, bit errors in a ciphertext segment affect the decryption of the next b/s (rounded up to the nearest integer) ciphertext segments. A bit error may occur, independently, in any bit position in these decrypted segments, with an expected error rate of fifty percent.

Similarly, for the CTR mode, if there is a bit error in a counter block, then a bit error may occur, independently, in any bit position of the decryption of the corresponding ciphertext, with an expected error rate of fifty percent.

Bit errors in IVs also affect the decryption process. In the OFB mode, bit errors in the IV affect the decryption of every ciphertext block. In the CFB mode, bit errors in the IV affect, at a minimum, the decryption of the first ciphertext segment, and possibly successive ciphertext segments, depending on the bit position of the rightmost bit error in the IV. (In general, a bit error in the ith most significant bit position affects the decryptions of the first i/s (rounding up) ciphertext segments.) For both the OFB and CFB modes, a bit error may occur, independently, in any bit position of the affected ciphertext blocks (or segments), with an expected error rate of fifty percent. In the CBC mode, if bit errors occur in the IV, then the first ciphertext block will be decrypted incorrectly, and bit errors will occur in exactly the same bit positions as in the IV; the decryptions of the other ciphertext blocks are not affected.

Consequently, for the CBC mode, the decryption of the first ciphertext block is vulnerable to the (deliberate) introduction of bit errors in specific bit positions of the IV if the integrity of the IV is not protected. Similarly, for the OFB and CTR modes, the decryption of any ciphertext block is vulnerable to the introduction of specific bit errors into that ciphertext block if its integrity is not protected. The same property also holds for the ciphertext segments in the CFB mode; however, for every ciphertext segment except the last one, the existence of such bit errors may be detected by their randomizing effect on the decryption of the succeeding ciphertext segment.

21

Table D.1 summarizes the effects of bit errors in a ciphertext block or IV on the decryption of the ciphertext for each of the five confidentiality modes.

Table D.1e five confidentiality modes.

Table D.2: Summary of Effect of Bit Errors on Decryption

Mode	Effect of Bit Errors in C_j	Effect of Bit Errors in the IV
ECB	RBE in the decryption of C_j	Not applicable
CBC	RBE in the decryption of C_j SBE in the decryption of C_{j+1}	SBE in the decryption of C_1
CFB	SBE in the decryption of C_j RBE in the decryption of $C_{j+1}, \ldots, C_{j+b/s}$	RBE in the decryption of $C_1, C_2, \ldots, C_j$ for some j between 1 and b/s
OFB	SBE in the decryption of C_j	RBE in the decryption of $C_1, C_2, \ldots, C_n$
CTR	SBE in the decryption of C_j	Not applicable *

RBE: random bit errors, i.e., bit errors occur independently in any bit position with an expected probability of ½.
SBE: specific bit errors, i.e., bit errors occur in the same bit position(s) as the original bit error(s).
* Bit errors in the jth counter block, T_j, result in RBE in the decryption of C_j.

The deletion or insertion of bits into a ciphertext block (or segment) spoils the synchronization of the block (or segment) boundaries; in effect, bit errors may occur in the bit position of the inserted or deleted bit, and in every subsequent bit position. Therefore, the decryptions of the subsequent ciphertext blocks (or segments) will almost certainly be incorrect until the synchronization is restored. When the 1-bit CFB mode is used, then the synchronization is automatically restored $b+1$ positions after the inserted or deleted bit. For other values of s in the CFB mode, and for the other confidentiality modes in this recommendation, the synchronization must be restored externally.

Appendix E: Modes of Triple DES

FIPS Pub 46-3 [FIPS 46-3] specifies the Data Encryption Standard (DES) algorithm and approves its three-fold, compound operation that is specified in ANSI X9.52 [1]: the Triple Data Encryption Algorithm (TDEA). Essentially, the TDEA consists of the application of the forward DES algorithm, i.e, DES encryption, under one key, followed by the application of the inverse DES algorithm, i.e., DES decryption, under a second key, followed by the application of the forward DES algorithm under a third key. The TDEA is often called Triple DES.

FIPS Pub 46-3 also approves the seven modes of operation of Triple DES that are specified in ANSI X9.52. Four of those modes are equivalent to modes in this recommendation with the TDEA as the underlying block cipher. In particular, the TECB, TCBC, and TOFB modes in ANSI X9.52 are equivalent to the ECB, CBC, and OFB modes in this recommendation, with the TDEA as the underlying block cipher; the TCFB mode in ANSI X9.52 is equivalent to the CFB mode in this recommendation, with the TDEA as the underlying block cipher, provided that the possible choices of the parameter s (the segment size) are restricted to three values: 1, 8, and 64. The remaining three modes in ANSI X9.52 are TCBC-I, TCFB-P, and TOFB-I; they are mode variants that allow for interleaving or pipelining; this recommendation does not provide analogues of these three modes.

The Triple DES *modes* in ANSI X9.52 should not be used as the underlying block cipher algorithm for the modes in this recommendation. However, the Triple DES *algorithm*, i.e., TDEA, as described above, may be used as the underlying block cipher algorithm for the six modes in this recommendation. One of the resulting modes of Triple DES is new, i.e., not specified in ANSI X9.52: the CTR mode of the TDEA.

Appendix F: Example Vectors for Modes of Operation of the AES

In this appendix, three examples are provided for each of the modes in this recommendation with the AES algorithm [2] as the underlying block cipher: one example is given for each of the allowed key sizes (128, 192, and 256 bits). Some intermediate results are presented. For the five confidentiality modes, examples are provided for both encryption and decryption. Examples are provided for 1-bit, 8-bit, and 128 bit CFB. The plaintext for all but two of these examples is equivalent to the following string of hexadecimal characters, formatted into four 128 bit blocks:

```
6bc1bee22e409f96e93d7e117393172a
ae2d8a571e03ac9c9eb76fac45af8e51
30c81c46a35ce411e5fbc1191a0a52ef
f69f2445df4f9b17ad2b417be66c3710.
```

For the example of 1-bit CFB, the plaintext is the first 16 bits in the above string; for the example of 8-bit CFB, the plaintext is the first 18 octets in the above string. All strings are presented in hexadecimal notation, except in the example of 1-bit CFB, where the plaintext and ciphertext segments are single bits.

F.1   ECB Example Vectors

F.1.1   ECB-AES128.Encrypt
```
Key               2b7e151628aed2a6abf7158809cf4f3c
Block #1
Plaintext         6bc1bee22e409f96e93d7e117393172a
Input Block       6bc1bee22e409f96e93d7e117393172a
Output Block      3ad77bb40d7a3660a89ecaf32466ef97
Ciphertext        3ad77bb40d7a3660a89ecaf32466ef97
Block #2
Plaintext         ae2d8a571e03ac9c9eb76fac45af8e51
Input Block       ae2d8a571e03ac9c9eb76fac45af8e51
Output Block      f5d3d58503b9699de785895a96fdbaaf
Ciphertext        f5d3d58503b9699de785895a96fdbaaf
Block #3
Plaintext         30c81c46a35ce411e5fbc1191a0a52ef
Input Block       30c81c46a35ce411e5fbc1191a0a52ef
Output Block      43b1cd7f598ece23881b00e3ed030688
Ciphertext        43b1cd7f598ece23881b00e3ed030688
Block #4
Plaintext         f69f2445df4f9b17ad2b417be66c3710
Input Block       f69f2445df4f9b17ad2b417be66c3710
Output Block      7b0c785e27e8ad3f8223207104725dd4
Ciphertext        7b0c785e27e8ad3f8223207104725dd4
```

F.1.2   ECB-AES128.Decrypt
```
Key               2b7e151628aed2a6abf7158809cf4f3c
Block #1
Ciphertext        3ad77bb40d7a3660a89ecaf32466ef97
Input Block       3ad77bb40d7a3660a89ecaf32466ef97
```

24

```
Output Block      6bc1bee22e409f96e93d7e117393172a
Plaintext         6bc1bee22e409f96e93d7e117393172a
Block #2
Ciphertext        f5d3d58503b9699de785895a96fdbaaf
Input Block       f5d3d58503b9699de785895a96fdbaaf
Output Block      ae2d8a571e03ac9c9eb76fac45af8e51
Plaintext         ae2d8a571e03ac9c9eb76fac45af8e51
Block #3
Ciphertext        43b1cd7f598ece23881b00e3ed030688
Input Block       43b1cd7f598ece23881b00e3ed030688
Output Block      30c81c46a35ce411e5fbc1191a0a52ef
Plaintext         30c81c46a35ce411e5fbc1191a0a52ef
Block #4
Ciphertext        7b0c785e27e8ad3f8223207104725dd4
Input Block       7b0c785e27e8ad3f8223207104725dd4
Output Block      f69f2445df4f9b17ad2b417be66c3710
Plaintext         f69f2445df4f9b17ad2b417be66c3710
```

F.1.3   ECB-AES192.Encrypt
```
Key               8e73b0f7da0e6452c810f32b809079e562f8ead2522c6b7b
Block #1
Plaintext         6bc1bee22e409f96e93d7e117393172a
Input Block       6bc1bee22e409f96e93d7e117393172a
Output Block      bd334f1d6e45f25ff712a214571fa5cc
Ciphertext        bd334f1d6e45f25ff712a214571fa5cc
Block #2
Plaintext         ae2d8a571e03ac9c9eb76fac45af8e51
Input Block       ae2d8a571e03ac9c9eb76fac45af8e51
Output Block      974104846d0ad3ad7734ecb3ecee4eef
Ciphertext        974104846d0ad3ad7734ecb3ecee4eef
Block #3
Plaintext         30c81c46a35ce411e5fbc1191a0a52ef
Input Block       30c81c46a35ce411e5fbc1191a0a52ef
Output Block      ef7afd2270e2e60adce0ba2face6444e
Ciphertext        ef7afd2270e2e60adce0ba2face6444e
Block #4
Plaintext         f69f2445df4f9b17ad2b417be66c3710
Input Block       f69f2445df4f9b17ad2b417be66c3710
Output Block      9a4b41ba738d6c72fb16691603c18e0e
Ciphertext        9a4b41ba738d6c72fb16691603c18e0e
```

F.1.4   ECB-AES192.Decrypt
```
Key               8e73b0f7da0e6452c810f32b809079e562f8ead2522c6b7b
Block #1
Ciphertext        bd334f1d6e45f25ff712a214571fa5cc
Input Block       bd334f1d6e45f25ff712a214571fa5cc
Output Block      6bc1bee22e409f96e93d7e117393172a
Plaintext         6bc1bee22e409f96e93d7e117393172a
Block #2
Ciphertext        974104846d0ad3ad7734ecb3ecee4eef
Input Block       974104846d0ad3ad7734ecb3ecee4eef
Output Block      ae2d8a571e03ac9c9eb76fac45af8e51
Plaintext         ae2d8a571e03ac9c9eb76fac45af8e51
```

```
Block #3
Ciphertext        ef7afd2270e2e60adce0ba2face6444e
Input Block       ef7afd2270e2e60adce0ba2face6444e
Output Block      30c81c46a35ce411e5fbc1191a0a52ef
Plaintext         30c81c46a35ce411e5fbc1191a0a52ef
Block #4
Ciphertext        9a4b41ba738d6c72fb16691603c18e0e
Input Block       9a4b41ba738d6c72fb16691603c18e0e
Output Block      f69f2445df4f9b17ad2b417be66c3710
Plaintext         f69f2445df4f9b17ad2b417be66c3710
```

F.1.5   ECB-AES256.Encrypt

```
Key               603deb1015ca71be2b73aef0857d7781
                  1f352c073b6108d72d9810a30914dff4
Block #1
Plaintext         6bc1bee22e409f96e93d7e117393172a
Input Block       6bc1bee22e409f96e93d7e117393172a
Output Block      f3eed1bdb5d2a03c064b5a7e3db181f8
Ciphertext        f3eed1bdb5d2a03c064b5a7e3db181f8
Block #2
Plaintext         ae2d8a571e03ac9c9eb76fac45af8e51
Input Block       ae2d8a571e03ac9c9eb76fac45af8e51
Output Block      591ccb10d410ed26dc5ba74a31362870
Ciphertext        591ccb10d410ed26dc5ba74a31362870
Block #3
Plaintext         30c81c46a35ce411e5fbc1191a0a52ef
Input Block       30c81c46a35ce411e5fbc1191a0a52ef
Output Block      b6ed21b99ca6f4f9f153e7b1beafed1d
Ciphertext        b6ed21b99ca6f4f9f153e7b1beafed1d
Block #4
Plaintext         f69f2445df4f9b17ad2b417be66c3710
Input Block       f69f2445df4f9b17ad2b417be66c3710
Output Block      23304b7a39f9f3ff067d8d8f9e24ecc7
Ciphertext        23304b7a39f9f3ff067d8d8f9e24ecc7
```

F.1.6   ECB-AES256.Decrypt

```
Key               603deb1015ca71be2b73aef0857d7781
                  1f352c073b6108d72d9810a30914dff4
Block #1
Ciphertext        f3eed1bdb5d2a03c064b5a7e3db181f8
Input Block       f3eed1bdb5d2a03c064b5a7e3db181f8
Output Block      6bc1bee22e409f96e93d7e117393172a
Plaintext         6bc1bee22e409f96e93d7e117393172a
Block #2
Ciphertext        591ccb10d410ed26dc5ba74a31362870
Input Block       591ccb10d410ed26dc5ba74a31362870
Output Block      ae2d8a571e03ac9c9eb76fac45af8e51
Plaintext         ae2d8a571e03ac9c9eb76fac45af8e51
Block #3
Ciphertext        b6ed21b99ca6f4f9f153e7b1beafed1d
Input Block       b6ed21b99ca6f4f9f153e7b1beafed1d
Output Block      30c81c46a35ce411e5fbc1191a0a52ef
Plaintext         30c81c46a35ce411e5fbc1191a0a52ef
```

```
Block #4
Ciphertext      23304b7a39f9f3ff067d8d8f9e24ecc7
Input Block     23304b7a39f9f3ff067d8d8f9e24ecc7
Output Block    f69f2445df4f9b17ad2b417be66c3710
Plaintext       f69f2445df4f9b17ad2b417be66c3710
```

F.2   *CBC Example Vectors*

F.2.1   *CBC-AES128.Encrypt*
```
Key             2b7e151628aed2a6abf7158809cf4f3c
IV              000102030405060708090a0b0c0d0e0f
Block #1
Plaintext       6bc1bee22e409f96e93d7e117393172a
Input Block     6bc0bce12a459991e134741a7f9e1925
Output Block    7649abac8119b246cee98e9b12e9197d
Ciphertext      7649abac8119b246cee98e9b12e9197d
Block #2
Plaintext       ae2d8a571e03ac9c9eb76fac45af8e51
Input Block     d86421fb9f1a1eda505ee1375746972c
Output Block    5086cb9b507219ee95db113a917678b2
Ciphertext      5086cb9b507219ee95db113a917678b2
Block #3
Plaintext       30c81c46a35ce411e5fbc1191a0a52ef
Input Block     604ed7ddf32efdff7020d0238b7c2a5d
Output Block    73bed6b8e3c1743b7116e69e22229516
Ciphertext      73bed6b8e3c1743b7116e69e22229516
Block #4
Plaintext       f69f2445df4f9b17ad2b417be66c3710
Input Block     8521f2fd3c8eef2cdc3da7e5c44ea206
Output Block    3ff1caa1681fac09120eca307586e1a7
Ciphertext      3ff1caa1681fac09120eca307586e1a7
```

F.2.2   *CBC-AES128.Decrypt*
```
Key             2b7e151628aed2a6abf7158809cf4f3c
IV              000102030405060708090a0b0c0d0e0f
Block #1
Ciphertext      7649abac8119b246cee98e9b12e9197d
Input Block     7649abac8119b246cee98e9b12e9197d
Output Block    6bc0bce12a459991e134741a7f9e1925
Plaintext       6bc1bee22e409f96e93d7e117393172a
Block #2
Ciphertext      5086cb9b507219ee95db113a917678b2
Input Block     5086cb9b507219ee95db113a917678b2
Output Block    d86421fb9f1a1eda505ee1375746972c
Plaintext       ae2d8a571e03ac9c9eb76fac45af8e51
Block #3
Ciphertext      73bed6b8e3c1743b7116e69e22229516
Input Block     73bed6b8e3c1743b7116e69e22229516
Output Block    604ed7ddf32efdff7020d0238b7c2a5d
Plaintext       30c81c46a35ce411e5fbc1191a0a52ef
Block #4
Ciphertext      3ff1caa1681fac09120eca307586e1a7
Input Block     3ff1caa1681fac09120eca307586e1a7
```

```
Output Block        8521f2fd3c8eef2cdc3da7e5c44ea206
Plaintext           f69f2445df4f9b17ad2b417be66c3710
```

F.2.3   CBC-AES192.Encrypt

```
Key            8e73b0f7da0e6452c810f32b809079e562f8ead2522c6b7b
IV             000102030405060708090a0b0c0d0e0f
Block #1
Plaintext      6bc1bee22e409f96e93d7e117393172a
Input Block    6bc0bce12a459991e134741a7f9e1925
Output Block   4f021db243bc633d7178183a9fa071e8
Ciphertext     4f021db243bc633d7178183a9fa071e8
Block #2
Plaintext      ae2d8a571e03ac9c9eb76fac45af8e51
Input Block    e12f97e55dbfcfa1efcf7796da0fffb9
Output Block   b4d9ada9ad7dedf4e5e738763f69145a
Ciphertext     b4d9ada9ad7dedf4e5e738763f69145a
Block #3
Plaintext      30c81c46a35ce411e5fbc1191a0a52ef
Input Block    8411b1ef0e2109e5001cf96f256346b5
Output Block   571b242012fb7ae07fa9baac3df102e0
Ciphertext     571b242012fb7ae07fa9baac3df102e0
Block #4
Plaintext      f69f2445df4f9b17ad2b417be66c3710
Input Block    a1840065cdb4e1f7d282fbd7db9d35f0
Output Block   08b0e27988598881d920a9e64f5615cd
Ciphertext     08b0e27988598881d920a9e64f5615cd
```

F.2.4   CBC-AES192.Decrypt

```
Key            8e73b0f7da0e6452c810f32b809079e562f8ead2522c6b7b
IV             000102030405060708090a0b0c0d0e0f
Block #1
Ciphertext     4f021db243bc633d7178183a9fa071e8
Input Block    4f021db243bc633d7178183a9fa071e8
Output Block   6bc0bce12a459991e134741a7f9e1925
Plaintext      6bc1bee22e409f96e93d7e117393172a
Block #2
Ciphertext     b4d9ada9ad7dedf4e5e738763f69145a
Input Block    b4d9ada9ad7dedf4e5e738763f69145a
Output Block   e12f97e55dbfcfa1efcf7796da0fffb9
Plaintext      ae2d8a571e03ac9c9eb76fac45af8e51
Block #3
Ciphertext     571b242012fb7ae07fa9baac3df102e0
Input Block    571b242012fb7ae07fa9baac3df102e0
Output Block   8411b1ef0e2109e5001cf96f256346b5
Plaintext      30c81c46a35ce411e5fbc1191a0a52ef
Block #4
Ciphertext     08b0e27988598881d920a9e64f5615cd
Input Block    08b0e27988598881d920a9e64f5615cd
Output Block   a1840065cdb4e1f7d282fbd7db9d35f0
Plaintext      f69f2445df4f9b17ad2b417be66c3710
```

F.2.5   CBC-AES256.Encrypt

```
Key            603deb1015ca71be2b73aef0857d7781
```

```
                    1f352c073b6108d72d9810a30914dff4
IV                  000102030405060708090a0b0c0d0e0f
Block #1
Plaintext           6bc1bee22e409f96e93d7e117393172a
Input Block         6bc0bce12a459991e134741a7f9e1925
Output Block        f58c4c04d6e5f1ba779eabfb5f7bfbd6
Ciphertext          f58c4c04d6e5f1ba779eabfb5f7bfbd6
Block #2
Plaintext           ae2d8a571e03ac9c9eb76fac45af8e51
Input Block         5ba1c653c8e65d26e929c4571ad47587
Output Block        9cfc4e967edb808d679f777bc6702c7d
Ciphertext          9cfc4e967edb808d679f777bc6702c7d
Block #3
Plaintext           30c81c46a35ce411e5fbc1191a0a52ef
Input Block         ac3452d0dd87649c8264b662dc7a7e92
Output Block        39f23369a9d9bacfa530e26304231461
Ciphertext          39f23369a9d9bacfa530e26304231461
Block #4
Plaintext           f69f2445df4f9b17ad2b417be66c3710
Input Block         cf6d172c769621d8081ba318e24f2371
Output Block        b2eb05e2c39be9fcda6c19078c6a9d1b
Ciphertext          b2eb05e2c39be9fcda6c19078c6a9d1b
```

F.2.6   CBC-AES256.Decrypt

```
Key                 603deb1015ca71be2b73aef0857d7781
                    1f352c073b6108d72d9810a30914dff4
IV                  000102030405060708090a0b0c0d0e0f
Block #1
Ciphertext          f58c4c04d6e5f1ba779eabfb5f7bfbd6
Input Block         f58c4c04d6e5f1ba779eabfb5f7bfbd6
Output Block        6bc0bce12a459991e134741a7f9e1925
Plaintext           6bc1bee22e409f96e93d7e117393172a
Block #2
Ciphertext          9cfc4e967edb808d679f777bc6702c7d
Input Block         9cfc4e967edb808d679f777bc6702c7d
Output Block        5ba1c653c8e65d26e929c4571ad47587
Plaintext           ae2d8a571e03ac9c9eb76fac45af8e51
Block #3
Ciphertext          39f23369a9d9bacfa530e26304231461
Input Block         39f23369a9d9bacfa530e26304231461
Output Block        ac3452d0dd87649c8264b662dc7a7e92
Plaintext           30c81c46a35ce411e5fbc1191a0a52ef
Block #4
Ciphertext          b2eb05e2c39be9fcda6c19078c6a9d1b
Input Block         b2eb05e2c39be9fcda6c19078c6a9d1b
Output Block        cf6d172c769621d8081ba318e24f2371
Plaintext           f69f2445df4f9b17ad2b417be66c3710
```

F.3   CFB Example Vectors

F.3.1   CFB1-AES128.Encrypt

```
Key                 2b7e151628aed2a6abf7158809cf4f3c
IV                  000102030405060708090a0b0c0d0e0f
```

```
Segment #1
Input Block      000102030405060708090a0b0c0d0e0f
Output Block     50fe67cc996d32b6da0937e99bafec60
Plaintext        0
Ciphertext       0
Segment #2
Input Block      00020406080a0c0e10121416181a1c1e
Output Block     19cf576c7596e702f298b35666955c79
Plaintext        1
Ciphertext       1
Segment #3
Input Block      0004080c1014181c2024282c3034383d
Output Block     59e17759acd02b801fa321ea059e331f
Plaintext        1
Ciphertext       1
Segment #4
Input Block      0008101820283038404850586068707b
Output Block     71f415b0cc109e8b0faa14ab740c22f4
Plaintext        0
Ciphertext       0
Segment #5
Input Block      00102030405060708090a0b0c0d0e0f6
Output Block     3fb76d3d1048179964597a0f64d5adad
Plaintext        1
Ciphertext       1
Segment #6
Input Block      0020406080a0c0e10121416181a1c1ed
Output Block     4c943b4bac54ab974e3e52326d29aaa1
Plaintext        0
Ciphertext       0
Segment #7
Input Block      004080c1014181c2024282c3034383da
Output Block     c94da41eb3d3acf1993a512ab1e8203f
Plaintext        1
Ciphertext       0
Segment #8
Input Block      008101820283038404850586068707b4
Output Block     e07f5e98778f75dbb2691c3f582c3953
Plaintext        1
Ciphertext       0
Segment #9
Input Block      0102030405060708090a0b0c0d0e0f68
Output Block     02ef5fc8961efcce8568bc0731262dc7
Plaintext        1
Ciphertext       1
Segment #10
Input Block      020406080a0c0e10121416181a1c1ed1
Output Block     9f5a30367065efbe914b53698c8716b7
Plaintext        1
Ciphertext       0
Segment #11
Input Block      04080c1014181c2024282c3034383da2
Output Block     d018cfb81d0580edbff955ed74d382db
Plaintext        0
```

30

```
Ciphertext      1
Segment #12
Input Block     0810182028303840485058606870 7b45
Output Block    81272ab351e08e0b695b94b8164d86f4
Plaintext       0
Ciphertext      1
Segment #13
Input Block     1020304050607080909a0b0c0d0e0f68b
Output Block    094d33f856483d3fa01ba94f7e5ab3e7
Plaintext       0
Ciphertext      0
Segment #14
Input Block     20406080a0c0e10121416181a1c1ed16
Output Block    609900ad61923c8c102cd8d0d7947a2c
Plaintext       0
Ciphertext      0
Segment #15
Input Block     4080c1014181c2024282c3034383da2c
Output Block    9e5a154de966ab4db9c88b22a398134e
Plaintext       0
Ciphertext      1
Segment #16
Input Block     8101820283038404850586068707b459
Output Block    7fe16252b338bc4de3725c4156dfed20
Plaintext       1
Ciphertext      1
```

F.3.2   CFB1-AES128.Decrypt

```
Key             2b7e151628aed2a6abf7158809cf4f3c
IV              000102030405060708090a0b0c0d0e0f
Segment #1
Input Block     000102030405060708090a0b0c0d0e0f
Output Block    50fe67cc996d32b6da0937e99bafec60
Ciphertext      0
Plaintext       0
Segment #2
Input Block     00020406080a0c0e10121416181a1c1e
Output Block    19cf576c7596e702f298b35666955c79
Ciphertext      1
Plaintext       1
Segment #3
Input Block     0004080c1014181c2024282c3034383d
Output Block    59e17759acd02b801fa321ea059e331f
Ciphertext      1
Plaintext       1
Segment #4
Input Block     0008101820283038404850586068707b
Output Block    71f415b0cc109e8b0faa14ab740c22f4
Ciphertext      0
Plaintext       0
Segment #5
Input Block     00102030405060708090a0b0c0d0e0f6
Output Block    3fb76d3d1048179964597a0f64d5adad
```

31

```
Ciphertext        1
Plaintext         1
Segment #6
Input Block       0020406080a0c0e10121416181a1c1ed
Output Block      4c943b4bac54ab974e3e52326d29aaa1
Ciphertext        0
Plaintext         0
Segment #7
Input Block       004080c1014181c2024282c3034383da
Output Block      c94da41eb3d3acf1993a512ab1e8203f
Ciphertext        0
Plaintext         1
Segment #8
Input Block       0081018202830384048504850586068707b4
Output Block      e07f5e98778f75dbb2691c3f582c3953
Ciphertext        0
Plaintext         1
Segment #9
Input Block       0102030405060708090a0b0c0d0e0f68
Output Block      02ef5fc8961efcce8568bc0731262dc7
Ciphertext        1
Plaintext         1
Segment #10
Input Block       020406080a0c0e10121416181a1c1ed1
Output Block      9f5a30367065efbe914b53698c8716b7
Ciphertext        0
Plaintext         1
Segment #11
Input Block       04080c1014181c2024282c3034383da2
Output Block      d018cfb81d0580edbff955ed74d382db
Ciphertext        1
Plaintext         0
Segment #12
Input Block       081018202830384048504850586068707b45
Output Block      81272ab351e08e0b695b94b8164d86f4
Ciphertext        1
Plaintext         0
Segment #13
Input Block       102030405060708090a0b0c0d0e0f68b
Output Block      094d33f856483d3fa01ba94f7e5ab3e7
Ciphertext        0
Plaintext         0
Segment #14
Input Block       20406080a0c0e10121416181a1c1ed16
Output Block      609900ad61923c8c102cd8d0d7947a2c
Ciphertext        0
Plaintext         0
Segment #15
Input Block       4080c1014181c2024282c3034383da2c
Output Block      9e5a154de966ab4db9c88b22a398134e
Ciphertext        1
Plaintext         0
Segment #16
Input Block       81018202830384048504850586068707b459
```

```
Output Block        7fe16252b338bc4de3725c4156dfed20
Ciphertext          1
Plaintext           1
```

F.3.3   CFB1-AES192.Encrypt

```
Key                 8e73b0f7da0e6452c810f32b809079e562f8ead2522c6b7b
IV                  000102030405060708090a0b0c0d0e0f
Segment #1
Input Block         000102030405060708090a0b0c0d0e0f
Output Block        a609b38df3b1133dddff2718ba09565e
Plaintext           0
Ciphertext          1
Segment #2
Input Block         00020406080a0c0e10121416181a1c1f
Output Block        a0e2bee6eb1734379bd4908be6a991a0
Plaintext           1
Ciphertext          0
Segment #3
Input Block         0004080c1014181c2024282c3034383e
Output Block        b1a1766bedec7ee3ba9cd3f34fbed4c6
Plaintext           1
Ciphertext          0
Segment #4
Input Block         0008101820283038404850586068707c
Output Block        b294ae5f393ae0179e6d3d8c45a7a4b9
Plaintext           0
Ciphertext          1
Segment #5
Input Block         00102030405060708090a0b0c0d0e0f9
Output Block        f0f703ff5d0634aa8aee7f1e26aafca3
Plaintext           1
Ciphertext          0
Segment #6
Input Block         0020406080a0c0e10121416181a1c1f2
Output Block        4d67df426abdb8c89e7de9fb3069d8be
Plaintext           0
Ciphertext          0
Segment #7
Input Block         004080c1014181c2024282c3034383e4
Output Block        30bc892338dfa10664118b9f4ba348d2
Plaintext           1
Ciphertext          1
Segment #8
Input Block         0081018202830384048505860 68707c9
Output Block        763ad8c63ed78d66452bb44c8bb7a8c8
Plaintext           1
Ciphertext          1
Segment #9
Input Block         0102030405060708090a0b0c0d0e0f93
Output Block        bfc36f5cfbc1306859b48f8fa62a43df
Plaintext           1
Ciphertext          0
Segment #10
```

33

```
Input Block       020406080a0c0e10121416181a1c1f26
Output Block      16e27adac112a0bf6a69c95cbdf584a3
Plaintext         1
Ciphertext        1
Segment #11
Input Block       04080c1014181c2024282c3034383e4d
Output Block      1e9d21c3da3de9186251160045756ce0
Plaintext         0
Ciphertext        0
Segment #12
Input Block       0810182028303840485058606870 7c9a
Output Block      b836e0f661b51d8bd38c448e0e5a11bb
Plaintext         0
Ciphertext        1
Segment #13
Input Block       102030405060708090a0b0c0d0e0f935
Output Block      c5efcdd09dbb92d1faada8f6c9bab052
Plaintext         0
Ciphertext        1
Segment #14
Input Block       20406080a0c0e10121416181a1c1f26b
Output Block      7c99710018d88e40bd4ac8f1b2bf4dbb
Plaintext         0
Ciphertext        0
Segment #15
Input Block       4080c1014181c2024282c3034383e4d6
Output Block      173bcd8b4dad60ae6646813fdcb81f5b
Plaintext         0
Ciphertext        0
Segment #16
Input Block       8101820283038404850586068707c9ac
Output Block      09844c6d2272d148d5af1c7bf01bb439
Plaintext         1
Ciphertext        1
```

F.3.4 CFB1-AES192.Decrypt

```
Key        8e73b0f7da0e6452c810f32b809079e562f8ead2522c6b7b
IV         000102030405060708090a0b0c0d0e0f
Segment #1
Input Block       000102030405060708090a0b0c0d0e0f
Output Block      a609b38df3b1133dddff2718ba09565e
Ciphertext        1
Plaintext         0
Segment #2
Input Block       00020406080a0c0e10121416181a1c1f
Output Block      a0e2bee6eb1734379bd4908be6a991a0
Ciphertext        0
Plaintext         1
Segment #3
Input Block       0004080c1014181c2024282c3034383e
Output Block      b1a1766bedec7ee3ba9cd3f34fbed4c6
Ciphertext        0
Plaintext         1
```

```
Segment #4
Input Block     0008101820283038404850586068707c
Output Block    b294ae5f393ae0179e6d3d8c45a7a4b9
Ciphertext      1
Plaintext       0
Segment #5
Input Block     00102030405060708090a0b0c0d0e0f9
Output Block    f0f703ff5d0634aa8aee7f1e26aafca3
Ciphertext      0
Plaintext       1
Segment #6
Input Block     0020406080a0c0e10121416181a1c1f2
Output Block    4d67df426abdb8c89e7de9fb3069d8be
Ciphertext      0
Plaintext       0
Segment #7
Input Block     004080c1014181c2024282c3034383e4
Output Block    30bc892338dfa10664118b9f4ba348d2
Ciphertext      1
Plaintext       1
Segment #8
Input Block     0081018202830384048505860687 07c9
Output Block    763ad8c63ed78d66452bb44c8bb7a8c8
Ciphertext      1
Plaintext       1
Segment #9
Input Block     01020304050607 08090a0b0c0d0e0f93
Output Block    bfc36f5cfbc1306859b48f8fa62a43df
Ciphertext      0
Plaintext       1
Segment #10
Input Block     020406080a0c0e10121416181a1c1f26
Output Block    16e27adac112a0bf6a69c95cbdf584a3
Ciphertext      1
Plaintext       1
Segment #11
Input Block     04080c1014181c2024282c3034383e4d
Output Block    1e9d21c3da3de9186251160045756ce0
Ciphertext      0
Plaintext       0
Segment #12
Input Block     08101820283038404850586068707c9a
Output Block    b836e0f661b51d8bd38c448e0e5a11bb
Ciphertext      1
Plaintext       0
Segment #13
Input Block     102030405060708090a0b0c0d0e0f935
Output Block    c5efcdd09dbb92d1faada8f6c9bab052
Ciphertext      1
Plaintext       0
Segment #14
Input Block     20406080a0c0e10121416181a1c1f26b
Output Block    7c99710018d88e40bd4ac8f1b2bf4dbb
Ciphertext      0
```

```
Plaintext        0
Segment #15
Input Block      4080c1014181c2024282c3034383e4d6
Output Block     173bcd8b4dad60ae6646813fdcb81f5b
Ciphertext       0
Plaintext        0
Segment #16
Input Block      81018202830384048505860687070c9ac
Output Block     09844c6d2272d148d5af1c7bf01bb439
Ciphertext       1
Plaintext        1
```

F.3.5   CFB1-AES256.Encrypt

```
Key              603deb1015ca71be2b73aef0857d7781
                 1f352c073b6108d72d9810a30914dff4
IV               000102030405060708090a0b0c0d0e0f
Segment #1
Input Block      000102030405060708090a0b0c0d0e0f
Output Block     b7bf3a5df43989dd97f0fa97ebce2f4a
Plaintext        0
Ciphertext       1
Segment #2
Input Block      00020406080a0c0e10121416181a1c1f
Output Block     ee93d380e0f01117fffd78017599514a
Plaintext        1
Ciphertext       0
Segment #3
Input Block      0004080c1014181c2024282c3034383e
Output Block     857749898b3602aad91e699911de89b0
Plaintext        1
Ciphertext       0
Segment #4
Input Block      0008101820283038404850586068707c
Output Block     dce81c80810e2ba343a6bb402716b7a8
Plaintext        0
Ciphertext       1
Segment #5
Input Block      00102030405060708090a0b0c0d0e0f9
Output Block     e5517bfcdccea00501350a601f754823
Plaintext        1
Ciphertext       0
Segment #6
Input Block      0020406080a0c0e10121416181a1c1f2
Output Block     15799c7f4081a78cc41f29955349c5a0
Plaintext        0
Ciphertext       0
Segment #7
Input Block      004080c1014181c2024282c3034383e4
Output Block     84d246bdb391f6a7979ff5ccb8467262
Plaintext        1
Ciphertext       0
Segment #8
Input Block      0081018202830384048505860687070c8
```

Output Block	bb9e05db9855a9e7e3837a648dd4c3b0
Plaintext	1
Ciphertext	0
Segment #9	
Input Block	01020304050607080 90a0b0c0d0e0f90
Output Block	a413c5714f70287dfcd943004bf7ac8e
Plaintext	1
Ciphertext	0
Segment #10	
Input Block	020406080a0c0e10121416181a1c1f20
Output Block	a7310abf87610d66edf6c892a84460d5
Plaintext	1
Ciphertext	0
Segment #11	
Input Block	04080c1014181c2024282c3034383e40
Output Block	8aec6712d89bd147c83b51d787b11399
Plaintext	0
Ciphertext	1
Segment #12	
Input Block	0810182028303840 4850586068707c81
Output Block	2ff05b620f68134f4ba92deffbfc93b2
Plaintext	0
Ciphertext	0
Segment #13	
Input Block	1020304050607080 90a0b0c0d0e0f902
Output Block	819208afd5284316065a76bead028ad3
Plaintext	0
Ciphertext	1
Segment #14	
Input Block	20406080a0c0e10121416181a1c1f205
Output Block	1914ed64b2115167ce2ca4c813da5245
Plaintext	0
Ciphertext	0
Segment #15	
Input Block	4080c1014181c2024282c3034383e40a
Output Block	638abae8724a954ae9e1e2e119deb6e1
Plaintext	0
Ciphertext	0
Segment #16	
Input Block	810182028303840 4850586068707c814
Output Block	2b4f488a3f958c52a3f1db2da938360e
Plaintext	1
Ciphertext	1

F.3.6   CFB1-AES256.Decrypt

Key	603deb1015ca71be2b73aef0857d7781
	1f352c073b6108d72d9810a30914dff4
IV	000102030405060708090a0b0c0d0e0f
Segment #1	
Input Block	000102030405060708090a0b0c0d0e0f
Output Block	b7bf3a5df43989dd97f0fa97ebce2f4a
Ciphertext	1
Plaintext	0

```
Segment #2
Input Block      00020406080a0c0e10121416181a1c1f
Output Block     ee93d380e0f01117fffd78017599514a
Ciphertext       0
Plaintext        1
Segment #3
Input Block      0004080c1014181c2024282c3034383e
Output Block     857749898b3602aad91e699911de89b0
Ciphertext       0
Plaintext        1
Segment #4
Input Block      0008101820283038404850586068707c
Output Block     dce81c80810e2ba343a6bb402716b7a8
Ciphertext       1
Plaintext        0
Segment #5
Input Block      00102030405060708090a0b0c0d0e0f9
Output Block     e5517bfcdccea00501350a601f754823
Ciphertext       0
Plaintext        1
Segment #6
Input Block      0020406080a0c0e10121416181a1c1f2
Output Block     15799c7f4081a78cc41f29955349c5a0
Ciphertext       0
Plaintext        0
Segment #7
Input Block      004080c1014181c2024282c3034383e4
Output Block     84d246bdb391f6a7979ff5ccb8467262
Ciphertext       0
Plaintext        1
Segment #8
Input Block      008101820283038404850586068707c8
Output Block     bb9e05db9855a9e7e3837a648dd4c3b0
Ciphertext       0
Plaintext        1
Segment #9
Input Block      0102030405060708090a0b0c0d0e0f90
Output Block     a413c5714f70287dfcd943004bf7ac8e
Ciphertext       0
Plaintext        1
Segment #10
Input Block      020406080a0c0e10121416181a1c1f20
Output Block     a7310abf87610d66edf6c892a84460d5
Ciphertext       0
Plaintext        1
Segment #11
Input Block      04080c1014181c2024282c3034383e40
Output Block     8aec6712d89bd147c83b51d787b11399
Ciphertext       1
Plaintext        0
Segment #12
Input Block      08101820283038404850586068707c81
Output Block     2ff05b620f68134f4ba92deffbfc93b2
Ciphertext       0
```

38

```
Plaintext        0
Segment #13
Input Block      10203040506070809 0a0b0c0d0e0f902
Output Block     819208afd5284316065a76bead028ad3
Ciphertext       1
Plaintext        0
Segment #14
Input Block      20406080a0c0e10121416181a1c1f205
Output Block     1914ed64b2115167ce2ca4c813da5245
Ciphertext       0
Plaintext 0
Segment #15
Input Block      4080c1014181c2024282c3034383e40a
Output Block     638abae8724a954ae9e1e2e119deb6e1
Ciphertext       0
Plaintext        0
Segment #16
Input Block      810182028303840485 0586068707c814
Output Block     2b4f488a3f958c52a3f1db2da938360e
Ciphertext       1
Plaintext        1
```

F.3.7   CFB8-AES128.Encrypt

```
Key              2b7e151628aed2a6abf7158809cf4f3c
IV               000102030405060708090a0b0c0d0e0f
Segment #1
Input Block      000102030405060708090a0b0c0d0e0f
Output Block     50fe67cc996d32b6da0937e99bafec60
Plaintext        6b
Ciphertext       3b
Segment #2
Input Block      0102030405060708090a0b0c0d0e0f3b
Output Block     b8eb865a2b026381abb1d6560ed20f68
Plaintext        c1
Ciphertext       79
Segment #3
Input Block      02030405060708090a0b0c0d0e0f3b79
Output Block     fce6033b4edce64cbaed3f61ff5b927c
Plaintext        be
Ciphertext       42
Segment #4
Input Block      030405060708090a0b0c0d0e0f3b7942
Output Block     ae4e5e7ffe805f7a4395b180004f8ca8
Plaintext        e2
Ciphertext       4c
Segment #5
Input Block      0405060708090a0b0c0d0e0f3b79424c
Output Block     b205eb89445b62116f1deb988a81e6dd
Plaintext        2e
Ciphertext       9c
Segment #6
Input Block      05060708090a0b0c0d0e0f3b79424c9c
Output Block     4d21d456a5e239064fff4be0c0f85488
```

```
Plaintext        40
Ciphertext       0d
Segment #7
Input Block      060708090a0b0c0d0e0f3b79424c9c0d
Output Block     4b2f5c3895b9efdc85ee0c5178c7fd33
Plaintext        9f
Ciphertext       d4
Segment #8
Input Block      0708090a0b0c0d0e0f3b79424c9c0dd4
Output Block     a0976d856da260a34104d1a80953db4c
Plaintext        96
Ciphertext       36
Segment #9
Input Block      08090a0b0c0d0e0f3b79424c9c0dd436
Output Block     53674e5890a2c71b0f6a27a094e5808c
Plaintext        e9
Ciphertext       ba
Segment #10
Input Block      090a0b0c0d0e0f3b79424c9c0dd436ba
Output Block     f34cd32ffed495f8bc8adba194eccb7a
Plaintext        3d
Ciphertext       ce
Segment #11
Input Block      0a0b0c0d0e0f3b79424c9c0dd436bace
Output Block     e08cf2407d7ed676c9049586f1d48ba6
Plaintext        7e
Ciphertext       9e
Segment #12
Input Block      0b0c0d0e0f3b79424c9c0dd436bace9e
Output Block     1f5c88a19b6ca28e99c9aeb8982a6dd8
Plaintext        11
Ciphertext       0e
Segment #13
Input Block      0c0d0e0f3b79424c9c0dd436bace9e0e
Output Block     a70e63df781cf395a208bd2365c8779b
Plaintext        73
Ciphertext       d4
Segment #14
Input Block      0d0e0f3b79424c9c0dd436bace9e0ed4
Output Block     cbcfe8b3bcf9ac202ce18420013319ab
Plaintext        93
Ciphertext       58
Segment #15
Input Block      0e0f3b79424c9c0dd436bace9e0ed458
Output Block     7d9fac6604b3c8c5b1f8c5a00956cf56
Plaintext        17
Ciphertext       6a
Segment #16
Input Block      0f3b79424c9c0dd436bace9e0ed4586a
Output Block     65c3fa64bf0343986825c636f4a1efd2
Plaintext        2a
Ciphertext       4f
Segment #17
Input Block      3b79424c9c0dd436bace9e0ed4586a4f
```

```
Output Block      9cff5e5ff4f554d56c924b9d6a6de21d
Plaintext         ae
Ciphertext        32
Segment #18
Input Block       79424c9c0dd436bace9e0ed4586a4f32
Output Block      946c3dc1584cc18400ecd8c6052c44b1
Plaintext         2d
Ciphertext        b9
```

F.3.8   CFB8-AES128.Decrypt

```
Key               2b7e151628aed2a6abf7158809cf4f3c
IV                000102030405060708090a0b0c0d0e0f
Segment #1
Input Block       000102030405060708090a0b0c0d0e0f
Output Block      50fe67cc996d32b6da0937e99bafec60
Ciphertext        3b
Plaintext         6b
Segment #2
Input Block       0102030405060708090a0b0c0d0e0f3b
Output Block      b8eb865a2b026381abb1d6560ed20f68
Ciphertext        79
Plaintext         c1
Segment #3
Input Block       02030405060708090a0b0c0d0e0f3b79
Output Block      fce6033b4edce64cbaed3f61ff5b927c
Ciphertext        42
Plaintext         be
Segment #4
Input Block       030405060708090a0b0c0d0e0f3b7942
Output Block      ae4e5e7ffe805f7a4395b180004f8ca8
Ciphertext        4c
Plaintext         e2
Segment #5
Input Block       0405060708090a0b0c0d0e0f3b79424c
Output Block      b205eb89445b62116f1deb988a81e6dd
Ciphertext        9c
Plaintext         2e
Segment #6
Input Block       05060708090a0b0c0d0e0f3b79424c9c
Output Block      4d21d456a5e239064fff4be0c0f85488
Ciphertext        0d
Plaintext         40
Segment #7
Input Block       060708090a0b0c0d0e0f3b79424c9c0d
Output Block      4b2f5c3895b9efdc85ee0c5178c7fd33
Ciphertext        d4
Plaintext         9f
Segment #8
Input Block       0708090a0b0c0d0e0f3b79424c9c0dd4
Output Block      a0976d856da260a34104d1a80953db4c
Ciphertext        36
Plaintext         96
Segment #9
```

```
Input Block      08090a0b0c0d0e0f3b79424c9c0dd436
Output Block     53674e5890a2c71b0f6a27a094e5808c
Ciphertext       ba
Plaintext        e9
Segment #10
Input Block      090a0b0c0d0e0f3b79424c9c0dd436ba
Output Block     f34cd32ffed495f8bc8adba194eccb7a
Ciphertext       ce
Plaintext        3d
Segment #11
Input Block      0a0b0c0d0e0f3b79424c9c0dd436bace
Output Block     e08cf2407d7ed676c9049586f1d48ba6
Ciphertext       9e
Plaintext        7e
Segment #12
Input Block      0b0c0d0e0f3b79424c9c0dd436bace9e
Output Block     1f5c88a19b6ca28e99c9aeb8982a6dd8
Ciphertext       0e
Plaintext        11
Segment #13
Input Block      0c0d0e0f3b79424c9c0dd436bace9e0e
Output Block     a70e63df781cf395a208bd2365c8779b
Ciphertext       d4
Plaintext        73
Segment #14
Input Block      0d0e0f3b79424c9c0dd436bace9e0ed4
Output Block     cbcfe8b3bcf9ac202ce18420013319ab
Ciphertext       58
Plaintext        93
Segment #15
Input Block      0e0f3b79424c9c0dd436bace9e0ed458
Output Block     7d9fac6604b3c8c5b1f8c5a00956cf56
Ciphertext       6a
Plaintext        17
Segment #16
Input Block      0f3b79424c9c0dd436bace9e0ed4586a
Output Block     65c3fa64bf0343986825c636f4a1efd2
Ciphertext       4f
Plaintext        2a
Segment #17
Input Block      3b79424c9c0dd436bace9e0ed4586a4f
Output Block     9cff5e5ff4f554d56c924b9d6a6de21d
Ciphertext       32
Plaintext        ae
Segment #18
Input Block      79424c9c0dd436bace9e0ed4586a4f32
Output Block     946c3dc1584cc18400ecd8c6052c44b1
Ciphertext       b9
Plaintext        2d
```

F.3.9   CFB8-AES192.Encrypt
```
Key              8e73b0f7da0e6452c810f32b809079e562f8ead2522c6b7b
```

```
IV                 000102030405060708090a0b0c0d0e0f
Segment #1
Input Block        000102030405060708090a0b0c0d0e0f
Output Block       a609b38df3b1133dddff2718ba09565e
Plaintext          6b
Ciphertext         cd
Segment #2
Input Block        0102030405060708090a0b0c0d0e0fcd
Output Block       63c82e99e7289617c49e6851e082142a
Plaintext          c1
Ciphertext         a2
Segment #3
Input Block        02030405060708090a0b0c0d0e0fcda2
Output Block       ec40a5497264bfb4d6820aaae73f75af
Plaintext          be
Ciphertext         52
Segment #4
Input Block        030405060708090a0b0c0d0e0fcda252
Output Block       fc011a96afe968c32bae6495173a9154
Plaintext          e2
Ciphertext         1e
Segment #5
Input Block        0405060708090a0b0c0d0e0fcda2521e
Output Block       de019e09ac995ba46a42916ef77d8fe5
Plaintext          2e
Ciphertext         f0
Segment #6
Input Block        05060708090a0b0c0d0e0fcda2521ef0
Output Block       e980477efb7f896e07c4a2d527e7b537
Plaintext          40
Ciphertext         a9
Segment #7
Input Block        060708090a0b0c0d0e0fcda2521ef0a9
Output Block       9a9a77b11709b36e08e9321ae8b1e539
Plaintext          9f
Ciphertext         05
Segment #8
Input Block        0708090a0b0c0d0e0fcda2521ef0a905
Output Block       5ca1d192a780fbca1471e10588593c7c
Plaintext          96
Ciphertext         ca
Segment #9
Input Block        08090a0b0c0d0e0fcda2521ef0a905ca
Output Block       addb26efd21de4d002474c7748e0bc1d
Plaintext          e9
Ciphertext         44
Segment #10
Input Block        090a0b0c0d0e0fcda2521ef0a905ca44
Output Block       f0c410ad6512c5177a5ee40a60de01b8
Plaintext          3d
Ciphertext         cd
Segment #11
Input Block        0a0b0c0d0e0fcda2521ef0a905ca44cd
Output Block       7bbf71f2b4f5cf68f3c0c1b9235dbd53
```

```
Plaintext        7e
Ciphertext       05
Segment #12
Input Block      0b0c0d0e0fcda2521ef0a905ca44cd05
Output Block     6dafb26e3c63b350811394b382e14d69
Plaintext        11
Ciphertext       7c
Segment #13
Input Block      0c0d0e0fcda2521ef0a905ca44cd057c
Output Block     ccd6e25255a80e9bdbec9fbc26e5fad6
Plaintext        73
Ciphertext       bf
Segment #14
Input Block      0d0e0fcda2521ef0a905ca44cd057cbf
Output Block     9e33550f6d47bda77f4f3108181ab21c
Plaintext        93
Ciphertext       0d
Segment #15
Input Block      0e0fcda2521ef0a905ca44cd057cbf0d
Output Block     50b3eae29a6623fbef6d726dbda675a8
Plaintext        17
Ciphertext       47
Segment #16
Input Block      0fcda2521ef0a905ca44cd057cbf0d47
Output Block     8a2a57d1b9158539ef7ff42b33bf0a4a
Plaintext        2a
Ciphertext       a0
Segment #17
Input Block      cda2521ef0a905ca44cd057cbf0d47a0
Output Block     c94e9102ac731d2f127b657d810ef5a8
Plaintext        ae
Ciphertext       67
Segment #18
Input Block      a2521ef0a905ca44cd057cbf0d47a067
Output Block     a765ed650568fbe386660def5f8d491d
Plaintext        2d
Ciphertext       8a
```

F.3.10   CFB8-AES192.Decrypt

```
Key              8e73b0f7da0e6452c810f32b809079e562f8ead2522c6b7b
IV               000102030405060708090a0b0c0d0e0f
Segment #1
Input Block      000102030405060708090a0b0c0d0e0f
Output Block     a609b38df3b1133dddff2718ba09565e
Ciphertext       cd
Plaintext        6b
Segment #2
Input Block      0102030405060708090a0b0c0d0e0fcd
Output Block     63c82e99e7289617c49e6851e082142a
Ciphertext       a2
Plaintext        c1
Segment #3
Input Block      020304050607080090a0b0c0d0e0fcda2
```

```
Output Block    ec40a5497264bfb4d6820aaae73f75af
Ciphertext      52
Plaintext       be
Segment #4
Input Block     030405060708090a0b0c0d0e0fcda252
Output Block    fc011a96afe968c32bae6495173a9154
Ciphertext      1e
Plaintext       e2
Segment #5
Input Block     0405060708090a0b0c0d0e0fcda2521e
Output Block    de019e09ac995ba46a42916ef77d8fe5
Ciphertext      f0
Plaintext       2e
Segment #6
Input Block     05060708090a0b0c0d0e0fcda2521ef0
Output Block    e980477efb7f896e07c4a2d527e7b537
Ciphertext      a9
Plaintext       40
Segment #7
Input Block     060708090a0b0c0d0e0fcda2521ef0a9
Output Block    9a9a77b11709b36e08e9321ae8b1e539
Ciphertext      05
Plaintext       9f
Segment #8
Input Block     0708090a0b0c0d0e0fcda2521ef0a905
Output Block    5ca1d192a780fbca1471e10588593c7c
Ciphertext      ca
Plaintext       96
Segment #9
Input Block     08090a0b0c0d0e0fcda2521ef0a905ca
Output Block    addb26efd21de4d002474c7748e0bc1d
Ciphertext      44
Plaintext       e9
Segment #10
Input Block     090a0b0c0d0e0fcda2521ef0a905ca44
Output Block    f0c410ad6512c5177a5ee40a60de01b8
Ciphertext      cd
Plaintext       3d
Segment #11
Input Block     0a0b0c0d0e0fcda2521ef0a905ca44cd
Output Block    7bbf71f2b4f5cf68f3c0c1b9235dbd53
Ciphertext      05
Plaintext       7e
Segment #12
Input Block     0b0c0d0e0fcda2521ef0a905ca44cd05
Output Block    6dafb26e3c63b350811394b382e14d69
Ciphertext      7c
Plaintext       11
Segment #13
Input Block     0c0d0e0fcda2521ef0a905ca44cd057c
Output Block    ccd6e25255a80e9bdbec9fbc26e5fad6
Ciphertext      bf
Plaintext       73
Segment #14
```

```
Input Block       0d0e0fcda2521ef0a905ca44cd057cbf
Output Block      9e33550f6d47bda77f4f3108181ab21c
Ciphertext        0d
Plaintext         93
Segment #15
Input Block       0e0fcda2521ef0a905ca44cd057cbf0d
Output Block      50b3eae29a6623fbef6d726dbda675a8
Ciphertext        47
Plaintext         17
Segment #16
Input Block       0fcda2521ef0a905ca44cd057cbf0d47
Output Block      8a2a57d1b9158539ef7ff42b33bf0a4a
Ciphertext        a0
Plaintext         2a
Segment #17
Input Block       cda2521ef0a905ca44cd057cbf0d47a0
Output Block      c94e9102ac731d2f127b657d810ef5a8
Ciphertext        67
Plaintext         ae
Segment #18
Input Block       a2521ef0a905ca44cd057cbf0d47a067
Output Block      a765ed650568fbe386660def5f8d491d
Ciphertext        8a
Plaintext         2d
```

F.3.11   CFB8-AES256.Encrypt

```
Key               603deb1015ca71be2b73aef0857d7781
                  1f352c073b6108d72d9810a30914dff4
IV                000102030405060708090a0b0c0d0e0f
Segment #1
Input Block       000102030405060708090a0b0c0d0e0f
Output Block      b7bf3a5df43989dd97f0fa97ebce2f4a
Plaintext         6b
Ciphertext        dc
Segment #2
Input Block       0102030405060708090a0b0c0d0e0fdc
Output Block      ded5faadb1068af80e774684b9f84870
Plaintext         c1
Ciphertext        1f
Segment #3
Input Block       02030405060708090a0b0c0d0e0fdc1f
Output Block      a41e327e5273366ce9403cdbdb92c1cc
Plaintext         be
Ciphertext        1a
Segment #4
Input Block       030405060708090a0b0c0d0e0fdc1f1a
Output Block      67938ae7d34df4ec2c0aec33eb98318f
Plaintext         e2
Ciphertext        85
Segment #5
Input Block       0405060708090a0b0c0d0e0fdc1f1a85
Output Block      0e8f2e31efff615d3c93946609808c37
Plaintext         2e
```

46

Ciphertext	20
Segment #6	
Input Block	05060708090a0b0c0d0e0fdc1f1a8520
Output Block	e648bb37a95c94c72784162a79dfe306
Plaintext	40
Ciphertext	a6
Segment #7	
Input Block	060708090a0b0c0d0e0fdc1f1a8520a6
Output Block	d278f3147290fc5dd0b7d2e82764a1fd
Plaintext	9f
Ciphertext	4d
Segment #8	
Input Block	0708090a0b0c0d0e0fdc1f1a8520a64d
Output Block	2388d255a3e8a8059675e3a7de19dceb
Plaintext	96
Ciphertext	b5
Segment #9	
Input Block	08090a0b0c0d0e0fdc1f1a8520a64db5
Output Block	b6b8008f6c6dc2d6144641ed2023f0f5
Plaintext	e9
Ciphertext	5f
Segment #10	
Input Block	090a0b0c0d0e0fdc1f1a8520a64db55f
Output Block	f18f88a7aa3e3a6167dd93fb1137713a
Plaintext	3d
Ciphertext	cc
Segment #11	
Input Block	0a0b0c0d0e0fdc1f1a8520a64db55fcc
Output Block	f46c5e67bff7c070b26c0318c52d0ccd
Plaintext	7e
Ciphertext	8a
Segment #12	
Input Block	0b0c0d0e0fdc1f1a8520a64db55fcc8a
Output Block	d4dceae622f8f21d27375d8c2c5f9fba
Plaintext	11
Ciphertext	c5
Segment #13	
Input Block	0c0d0e0fdc1f1a8520a64db55fcc8ac5
Output Block	27e9e0d0a016709cd3ae0b5a9a242e31
Plaintext	73
Ciphertext	54
Segment #14	
Input Block	0d0e0fdc1f1a8520a64db55fcc8ac554
Output Block	17f69d50ce64ba0d085de70b9030bbb2
Plaintext	93
Ciphertext	84
Segment #15	
Input Block	0e0fdc1f1a8520a64db55fcc8ac55484
Output Block	59106ee400d18e104337669628c33cdd
Plaintext	17
Ciphertext	4e
Segment #16	
Input Block	0fdc1f1a8520a64db55fcc8ac554844e
Output Block	a29c6ac87e2245ec0796772c1f5312a8

```
Plaintext            2a
Ciphertext           88
Segment #17
Input Block          dc1f1a8520a64db55fcc8ac554844e88
Output Block         397b98fa2ec0ff8cc0cd821909551c9e
Plaintext            ae
Ciphertext           97
Segment #18
Input Block          1f1a8520a64db55fcc8ac554844e8897
Output Block         2d2d6fe9aef72f7b914b623a9c7abd54
Plaintext            2d
Ciphertext           00
```

F.3.12   CFB8-AES256.Decrypt

```
Key                  603deb1015ca71be2b73aef0857d7781
                     1f352c073b6108d72d9810a30914dff4
IV                   000102030405060708090a0b0c0d0e0f
Segment #1
Input Block          000102030405060708090a0b0c0d0e0f
Output Block         b7bf3a5df43989dd97f0fa97ebce2f4a
Ciphertext           dc
Plaintext            6b
Segment #2
Input Block          0102030405060708090a0b0c0d0e0fdc
Output Block         ded5faadb1068af80e774684b9f84870
Ciphertext           1f
Plaintext            c1
Segment #3
Input Block          02030405060708090a0b0c0d0e0fdc1f
Output Block         a41e327e5273366ce9403cdbdb92c1cc
Ciphertext           1a
Plaintext            be
Segment #4
Input Block          030405060708090a0b0c0d0e0fdc1f1a
Output Block         67938ae7d34df4ec2c0aec33eb98318f
Ciphertext           85
Plaintext            e2
Segment #5
Input Block          0405060708090a0b0c0d0e0fdc1f1a85
Output Block         0e8f2e31efff615d3c93946609808c37
Ciphertext           20
Plaintext            2e
Segment #6
Input Block          05060708090a0b0c0d0e0fdc1f1a8520
Output Block         e648bb37a95c94c72784162a79dfe306
Ciphertext           a6
Plaintext            40
Segment #7
Input Block          060708090a0b0c0d0e0fdc1f1a8520a6
Output Block         d278f3147290fc5dd0b7d2e82764a1fd
Ciphertext           4d
Plaintext            9f
Segment #8
```

Input Block	0708090a0b0c0d0e0fdc1f1a8520a64d
Output Block	2388d255a3e8a8059675e3a7de19dceb
Ciphertext	b5
Plaintext	96
Segment #9	
Input Block	08090a0b0c0d0e0fdc1f1a8520a64db5
Output Block	b6b8008f6c6dc2d6144641ed2023f0f5
Ciphertext	5f
Plaintext	e9
Segment #10	
Input Block	090a0b0c0d0e0fdc1f1a8520a64db55f
Output Block	f18f88a7aa3e3a6167dd93fb1137713a
Ciphertext	cc
Plaintext	3d
Segment #11	
Input Block	0a0b0c0d0e0fdc1f1a8520a64db55fcc
Output Block	f46c5e67bff7c070b26c0318c52d0ccd
Ciphertext	8a
Plaintext	7e
Segment #12	
Input Block	0b0c0d0e0fdc1f1a8520a64db55fcc8a
Output Block	d4dceae622f8f21d27375d8c2c5f9fba
Ciphertext	c5
Plaintext	11
Segment #13	
Input Block	0c0d0e0fdc1f1a8520a64db55fcc8ac5
Output Block	27e9e0d0a016709cd3ae0b5a9a242e31
Ciphertext	54
Plaintext	73
Segment #14	
Input Block	0d0e0fdc1f1a8520a64db55fcc8ac554
Output Block	17f69d50ce64ba0d085de70b9030bbb2
Ciphertext	84
Plaintext	93
Segment #15	
Input Block	0e0fdc1f1a8520a64db55fcc8ac55484
Output Block	59106ee400d18e104337669628c33cdd
Ciphertext	4e
Plaintext	17
Segment #16	
Input Block	0fdc1f1a8520a64db55fcc8ac554844e
Output Block	a29c6ac87e2245ec0796772c1f5312a8
Ciphertext	88
Plaintext	2a
Segment #17	
Input Block	dc1f1a8520a64db55fcc8ac554844e88
Output Block	397b98fa2ec0ff8cc0cd821909551c9e
Ciphertext	97
Plaintext	ae
Segment #18	
Input Block	1f1a8520a64db55fcc8ac554844e8897
Output Block	2d2d6fe9aef72f7b914b623a9c7abd54
Ciphertext	00
Plaintext	2d

F.3.13   CFB128-AES128.Encrypt

```
Key                2b7e151628aed2a6abf7158809cf4f3c
IV                 000102030405060708090a0b0c0d0e0f
Segment #1
Input Block        000102030405060708090a0b0c0d0e0f
Output Block       50fe67cc996d32b6da0937e99bafec60
Plaintext          6bc1bee22e409f96e93d7e117393172a
Ciphertext         3b3fd92eb72dad20333449f8e83cfb4a
Segment #2
Input Block        3b3fd92eb72dad20333449f8e83cfb4a
Output Block       668bcf60beb005a35354a201dab36bda
Plaintext          ae2d8a571e03ac9c9eb76fac45af8e51
Ciphertext         c8a64537a0b3a93fcde3cdad9f1ce58b
Segment #3
Input Block        c8a64537a0b3a93fcde3cdad9f1ce58b
Output Block       16bd032100975551547b4de89daea630
Plaintext          30c81c46a35ce411e5fbc1191a0a52ef
Ciphertext         26751f67a3cbb140b1808cf187a4f4df
Segment #4
Input Block        26751f67a3cbb140b1808cf187a4f4df
Output Block       36d42170a312871947ef8714799bc5f6
Plaintext          f69f2445df4f9b17ad2b417be66c3710
Ciphertext         c04b05357c5d1c0eeac4c66f9ff7f2e6
```

F.3.14   CFB128-AES128.Decrypt

```
Key                2b7e151628aed2a6abf7158809cf4f3c
IV                 000102030405060708090a0b0c0d0e0f
Segment #1
Input Block        000102030405060708090a0b0c0d0e0f
Output Block       50fe67cc996d32b6da0937e99bafec60
Ciphertext         3b3fd92eb72dad20333449f8e83cfb4a
Plaintext          6bc1bee22e409f96e93d7e117393172a
Segment #2
Input Block        3b3fd92eb72dad20333449f8e83cfb4a
Output Block       668bcf60beb005a35354a201dab36bda
Ciphertext         c8a64537a0b3a93fcde3cdad9f1ce58b
Plaintext          ae2d8a571e03ac9c9eb76fac45af8e51
Segment #3
Input Block        c8a64537a0b3a93fcde3cdad9f1ce58b
Output Block       16bd032100975551547b4de89daea630
Ciphertext         26751f67a3cbb140b1808cf187a4f4df
Plaintext          30c81c46a35ce411e5fbc1191a0a52ef
Segment #4
Input Block        26751f67a3cbb140b1808cf187a4f4df
Output Block       36d42170a312871947ef8714799bc5f6
Ciphertext         c04b05357c5d1c0eeac4c66f9ff7f2e6
Plaintext          f69f2445df4f9b17ad2b417be66c3710
```

F.3.15   CFB128-AES192.Encrypt

```
Key                8e73b0f7da0e6452c810f32b809079e562f8ead2522c6b7b
IV                 000102030405060708090a0b0c0d0e0f
Segment #1
```

```
Input Block     000102030405060708090a0b0c0d0e0f
Output Block    a609b38df3b1133dddff2718ba09565e
Plaintext       6bc1bee22e409f96e93d7e117393172a
Ciphertext      cdc80d6fddf18cab34c25909c99a4174
Segment #2
Input Block     cdc80d6fddf18cab34c25909c99a4174
Output Block    c9e3f5289f149abd08ad44dc52b2b32b
Plaintext       ae2d8a571e03ac9c9eb76fac45af8e51
Ciphertext      67ce7f7f81173621961a2b70171d3d7a
Segment #3
Input Block     67ce7f7f81173621961a2b70171d3d7a
Output Block    1ed6965b76c76ca02d1dcef404f09626
Plaintext       30c81c46a35ce411e5fbc1191a0a52ef
Ciphertext      2e1e8a1dd59b88b1c8e60fed1efac4c9
Segment #4
Input Block     2e1e8a1dd59b88b1c8e60fed1efac4c9
Output Block    36c0bbd976ccd4b7ef85cec1be273eef
Plaintext       f69f2445df4f9b17ad2b417be66c3710
Ciphertext      c05f9f9ca9834fa042ae8fba584b09ff
```

F.3.16   CFB128-AES192.Decrypt

```
Key             8e73b0f7da0e6452c810f32b809079e562f8ead2522c6b7b
IV              000102030405060708090a0b0c0d0e0f
Segment #1
Input Block     000102030405060708090a0b0c0d0e0f
Output Block    a609b38df3b1133dddff2718ba09565e
Ciphertext      cdc80d6fddf18cab34c25909c99a4174
Plaintext       6bc1bee22e409f96e93d7e117393172a
Segment #2
Input Block     cdc80d6fddf18cab34c25909c99a4174
Output Block    c9e3f5289f149abd08ad44dc52b2b32b
Ciphertext      67ce7f7f81173621961a2b70171d3d7a
Plaintext       ae2d8a571e03ac9c9eb76fac45af8e51
Segment #3
Input Block     67ce7f7f81173621961a2b70171d3d7a
Output Block    1ed6965b76c76ca02d1dcef404f09626
Ciphertext      2e1e8a1dd59b88b1c8e60fed1efac4c9
Plaintext       30c81c46a35ce411e5fbc1191a0a52ef
Segment #4
Input Block     2e1e8a1dd59b88b1c8e60fed1efac4c9
Output Block    36c0bbd976ccd4b7ef85cec1be273eef
Ciphertext      c05f9f9ca9834fa042ae8fba584b09ff
Plaintext       f69f2445df4f9b17ad2b417be66c3710
```

F.3.17   CFB128-AES256.Encrypt

```
Key             603deb1015ca71be2b73aef0857d7781
                1f352c073b6108d72d9810a30914dff4
IV              000102030405060708090a0b0c0d0e0f
Segment #1
Input Block     000102030405060708090a0b0c0d0e0f
Output Block    b7bf3a5df43989dd97f0fa97ebce2f4a
Plaintext       6bc1bee22e409f96e93d7e117393172a
Ciphertext      dc7e84bfda79164b7ecd8486985d3860
```

51

```
Segment #2
Input Block      dc7e84bfda79164b7ecd8486985d3860
Output Block     97d26743252b1d54aca653cf744ace2a
Plaintext        ae2d8a571e03ac9c9eb76fac45af8e51
Ciphertext       39ffed143b28b1c832113c6331e5407b
Segment #3
Input Block      39ffed143b28b1c832113c6331e5407b
Output Block     efd80f62b6b9af8344c511b13c70b016
Plaintext        30c81c46a35ce411e5fbc1191a0a52ef
Ciphertext       df10132415e54b92a13ed0a8267ae2f9
Segment #4
Input Block      df10132415e54b92a13ed0a8267ae2f9
Output Block     833ca131c5f655ef8d1a2346b3ddd361
Plaintext        f69f2445df4f9b17ad2b417be66c3710
Ciphertext       75a385741ab9cef82031623d55b1e471
```

F.3.18   CFB128-AES256.Decrypt

```
Key              603deb1015ca71be2b73aef0857d7781
                 1f352c073b6108d72d9810a30914dff4
IV               000102030405060708090a0b0c0d0e0f
Segment #1
Input Block      000102030405060708090a0b0c0d0e0f
Output Block     b7bf3a5df43989dd97f0fa97ebce2f4a
Ciphertext       dc7e84bfda79164b7ecd8486985d3860
Plaintext        6bc1bee22e409f96e93d7e117393172a
Segment #2
Input Block      dc7e84bfda79164b7ecd8486985d3860
Output Block     97d26743252b1d54aca653cf744ace2a
Ciphertext       39ffed143b28b1c832113c6331e5407b
Plaintext        ae2d8a571e03ac9c9eb76fac45af8e51
Segment #3
Input Block      39ffed143b28b1c832113c6331e5407b
Output Block     efd80f62b6b9af8344c511b13c70b016
Ciphertext       df10132415e54b92a13ed0a8267ae2f9
Plaintext        30c81c46a35ce411e5fbc1191a0a52ef
Segment #4
Input Block      df10132415e54b92a13ed0a8267ae2f9
Output Block     833ca131c5f655ef8d1a2346b3ddd361
Ciphertext       75a385741ab9cef82031623d55b1e471
Plaintext        f69f2445df4f9b17ad2b417be66c3710
```

F.4   OFB Example Vectors

F.4.1   OFB-AES128.Encrypt

```
Key              2b7e151628aed2a6abf7158809cf4f3c
IV               000102030405060708090a0b0c0d0e0f
Block #1
Input Block      000102030405060708090a0b0c0d0e0f
Output Block     50fe67cc996d32b6da0937e99bafec60
Plaintext        6bc1bee22e409f96e93d7e117393172a
Ciphertext       3b3fd92eb72dad20333449f8e83cfb4a
Block #2
Input Block      50fe67cc996d32b6da0937e99bafec60
```

```
Output Block     d9a4dada0892239f6b8b3d7680e15674
Plaintext        ae2d8a571e03ac9c9eb76fac45af8e51
Ciphertext       7789508d16918f03f53c52dac54ed825
Block #3
Input Block      d9a4dada0892239f6b8b3d7680e15674
Output Block     a78819583f0308e7a6bf36b1386abf23
Plaintext        30c81c46a35ce411e5fbc1191a0a52ef
Ciphertext       9740051e9c5fecf64344f7a82260edcc
Block #4
Input Block      a78819583f0308e7a6bf36b1386abf23
Output Block     c6d3416d29165c6fcb8e51a227ba994e
Plaintext        f69f2445df4f9b17ad2b417be66c3710
Ciphertext       304c6528f659c77866a510d9c1d6ae5e
```

F.4.2   OFB-AES128.Decrypt

```
Key              2b7e151628aed2a6abf7158809cf4f3c
IV               000102030405060708090a0b0c0d0e0f
Block #1
Input Block      000102030405060708090a0b0c0d0e0f
Output Block     50fe67cc996d32b6da0937e99bafec60
Ciphertext       3b3fd92eb72dad20333449f8e83cfb4a
Plaintext        6bc1bee22e409f96e93d7e117393172a
Block #2
Input Block      50fe67cc996d32b6da0937e99bafec60
Output Block     d9a4dada0892239f6b8b3d7680e15674
Ciphertext       7789508d16918f03f53c52dac54ed825
Plaintext        ae2d8a571e03ac9c9eb76fac45af8e51
Block #3
Input Block      d9a4dada0892239f6b8b3d7680e15674
Output Block     a78819583f0308e7a6bf36b1386abf23
Ciphertext       9740051e9c5fecf64344f7a82260edcc
Plaintext        30c81c46a35ce411e5fbc1191a0a52ef
Block #4
Input Block      a78819583f0308e7a6bf36b1386abf23
Output Block     c6d3416d29165c6fcb8e51a227ba994e
Ciphertext       304c6528f659c77866a510d9c1d6ae5e
Plaintext        f69f2445df4f9b17ad2b417be66c3710
```

F.4.3   OFB-AES192.Encrypt

```
Key              8e73b0f7da0e6452c810f32b809079e562f8ead2522c6b7b
IV               000102030405060708090a0b0c0d0e0f
Block #1
Input Block      000102030405060708090a0b0c0d0e0f
Output Block     a609b38df3b1133dddff2718ba09565e
Plaintext        6bc1bee22e409f96e93d7e117393172a
Ciphertext       cdc80d6fddf18cab34c25909c99a4174
Block #2
Input Block      a609b38df3b1133dddff2718ba09565e
Output Block     52ef01da52602fe0975f78ac84bf8a50
Plaintext        ae2d8a571e03ac9c9eb76fac45af8e51
Ciphertext       fcc28b8d4c63837c09e81700c1100401
Block #3
Input Block      52ef01da52602fe0975f78ac84bf8a50
```

53

```
Output Block    bd5286ac63aabd7eb067ac54b553f71d
Plaintext       30c81c46a35ce411e5fbc1191a0a52ef
Ciphertext      8d9a9aeac0f6596f559c6d4daf59a5f2
Block #4
Input Block     bd5286ac63aabd7eb067ac54b553f71d
Output Block    9b00044d8885f729318713303fc0fe3a
Plaintext       f69f2445df4f9b17ad2b417be66c3710
Ciphertext      6d9f200857ca6c3e9cac524bd9acc92a
```

F.4.4   OFB-AES192.Decrypt

```
Key             8e73b0f7da0e6452c810f32b809079e562f8ead2522c6b7b
IV              000102030405060708090a0b0c0d0e0f
Block #1
Input Block     000102030405060708090a0b0c0d0e0f
Output Block    a609b38df3b1133dddff2718ba09565e
Ciphertext      cdc80d6fddf18cab34c25909c99a4174
Plaintext       6bc1bee22e409f96e93d7e117393172a
Block #2
Input Block     a609b38df3b1133dddff2718ba09565e
Output Block    52ef01da52602fe0975f78ac84bf8a50
Ciphertext      fcc28b8d4c63837c09e81700c1100401
Plaintext       ae2d8a571e03ac9c9eb76fac45af8e51
Block #3
Input Block     52ef01da52602fe0975f78ac84bf8a50
Output Block    bd5286ac63aabd7eb067ac54b553f71d
Ciphertext      8d9a9aeac0f6596f559c6d4daf59a5f2
Plaintext       30c81c46a35ce411e5fbc1191a0a52ef
Block #4
Input Block     bd5286ac63aabd7eb067ac54b553f71d
Output Block    9b00044d8885f729318713303fc0fe3a
Ciphertext      6d9f200857ca6c3e9cac524bd9acc92a
Plaintext       f69f2445df4f9b17ad2b417be66c3710
```

F.4.5   OFB-AES256.Encrypt

```
Key             603deb1015ca71be2b73aef0857d7781
                1f352c073b6108d72d9810a30914dff4
IV              000102030405060708090a0b0c0d0e0f
Block #1
Input Block     000102030405060708090a0b0c0d0e0f
Output Block    b7bf3a5df43989dd97f0fa97ebce2f4a
Plaintext       6bc1bee22e409f96e93d7e117393172a
Ciphertext      dc7e84bfda79164b7ecd8486985d3860
Block #2
Input Block     b7bf3a5df43989dd97f0fa97ebce2f4a
Output Block    e1c656305ed1a7a6563805746fe03edc
Plaintext       ae2d8a571e03ac9c9eb76fac45af8e51
Ciphertext      4febdc6740d20b3ac88f6ad82a4fb08d
Block #3
Input Block     e1c656305ed1a7a6563805746fe03edc
Output Block    41635be625b48afc1666dd42a09d96e7
Plaintext       30c81c46a35ce411e5fbc1191a0a52ef
Ciphertext      71ab47a086e86eedf39d1c5bba97c408
Block #4
```

```
Input Block      41635be625b48afc1666dd42a09d96e7
Output Block     f7b93058b8bce0fffea41bf0012cd394
Plaintext        f69f2445df4f9b17ad2b417be66c3710
Ciphertext       0126141d67f37be8538f5a8be740e484
```

F.4.6   OFB-AES256.Decrypt

```
Key              603deb1015ca71be2b73aef0857d7781
                 1f352c073b6108d72d9810a30914dff4
IV               000102030405060708090a0b0c0d0e0f
Block #1
Input Block      000102030405060708090a0b0c0d0e0f
Output Block     b7bf3a5df43989dd97f0fa97ebce2f4a
Ciphertext       dc7e84bfda79164b7ecd8486985d3860
Plaintext        6bc1bee22e409f96e93d7e117393172a
Block #2
Input Block      b7bf3a5df43989dd97f0fa97ebce2f4a
Output Block     e1c656305ed1a7a6563805746fe03edc
Ciphertext       4febdc6740d20b3ac88f6ad82a4fb08d
Plaintext        ae2d8a571e03ac9c9eb76fac45af8e51
Block #3
Input Block      e1c656305ed1a7a6563805746fe03edc
Output Block     41635be625b48afc1666dd42a09d96e7
Ciphertext       71ab47a086e86eedf39d1c5bba97c408
Plaintext        30c81c46a35ce411e5fbc1191a0a52ef
Block #4
Input Block      41635be625b48afc1666dd42a09d96e7
Output Block     f7b93058b8bce0fffea41bf0012cd394
Ciphertext       0126141d67f37be8538f5a8be740e484
Plaintext        f69f2445df4f9b17ad2b417be66c3710
```

F.5   CTR Example Vectors

F.5.1   CTR-AES128.Encrypt

```
Key              2b7e151628aed2a6abf7158809cf4f3c
Init. Counter    f0f1f2f3f4f5f6f7f8f9fafbfcfdfeff
Block #1
Input Block      f0f1f2f3f4f5f6f7f8f9fafbfcfdfeff
Output Block     ec8cdf7398607cb0f2d21675ea9ea1e4
Plaintext        6bc1bee22e409f96e93d7e117393172a
Ciphertext       874d6191b620e3261bef6864990db6ce
Block #2
Input Block      f0f1f2f3f4f5f6f7f8f9fafbfcfdff00
Output Block     362b7c3c6773516318a077d7fc5073ae
Plaintext        ae2d8a571e03ac9c9eb76fac45af8e51
Ciphertext       9806f66b7970fdff8617187bb9fffdff
Block #3
Input Block      f0f1f2f3f4f5f6f7f8f9fafbfcfdff01
Output Block     6a2cc3787889374fbeb4c81b17ba6c44
Plaintext        30c81c46a35ce411e5fbc1191a0a52ef
Ciphertext       5ae4df3edbd5d35e5b4f09020db03eab
Block #4
Input Block      f0f1f2f3f4f5f6f7f8f9fafbfcfdff02
Output Block     e89c399ff0f198c6d40a31db156cabfe
```

```
Plaintext      f69f2445df4f9b17ad2b417be66c3710
Ciphertext     1e031dda2fbe03d1792170a0f3009cee
```

F.5.2   CTR-AES128.Decrypt

```
Key               2b7e151628aed2a6abf7158809cf4f3c
Init. Counter     f0f1f2f3f4f5f6f7f8f9fafbfcfdfeff
Block #1
Input Block       f0f1f2f3f4f5f6f7f8f9fafbfcfdfeff
Output Block      ec8cdf7398607cb0f2d21675ea9ea1e4
Ciphertext        874d6191b620e3261bef6864990db6ce
Plaintext         6bc1bee22e409f96e93d7e117393172a
Block #2
Input Block       f0f1f2f3f4f5f6f7f8f9fafbfcfdff00
Output Block      362b7c3c6773516318a077d7fc5073ae
Ciphertext        9806f66b7970fdff8617187bb9fffdff
Plaintext         ae2d8a571e03ac9c9eb76fac45af8e51
Block #3
Input Block       f0f1f2f3f4f5f6f7f8f9fafbfcfdff01
Output Block      6a2cc3787889374fbeb4c81b17ba6c44
Ciphertext        5ae4df3edbd5d35e5b4f09020db03eab
Plaintext         30c81c46a35ce411e5fbc1191a0a52ef
Block #4
Input Block       f0f1f2f3f4f5f6f7f8f9fafbfcfdff02
Output Block      e89c399ff0f198c6d40a31db156cabfe
Ciphertext        1e031dda2fbe03d1792170a0f3009cee
Plaintext         f69f2445df4f9b17ad2b417be66c3710
```

F.5.3   CTR-AES192.Encrypt

```
Key               8e73b0f7da0e6452c810f32b809079e562f8ead2522c6b7b
Init. Counter     f0f1f2f3f4f5f6f7f8f9fafbfcfdfeff
Block #1
Input Block       f0f1f2f3f4f5f6f7f8f9fafbfcfdfeff
Output Block      717d2dc639128334a6167a488ded7921
Plaintext         6bc1bee22e409f96e93d7e117393172a
Ciphertext        1abc932417521ca24f2b0459fe7e6e0b
Block #2
Input Block       f0f1f2f3f4f5f6f7f8f9fafbfcfdff00
Output Block      a72eb3bb14a556734b7bad6ab16100c5
Plaintext         ae2d8a571e03ac9c9eb76fac45af8e51
Ciphertext        090339ec0aa6faefd5ccc2c6f4ce8e94
Block #3
Input Block       f0f1f2f3f4f5f6f7f8f9fafbfcfdff01
Output Block      2efeae2d72b722613446dc7f4c2af918
Plaintext         30c81c46a35ce411e5fbc1191a0a52ef
Ciphertext        1e36b26bd1ebc670d1bd1d665620abf7
Block #4
Input Block       f0f1f2f3f4f5f6f7f8f9fafbfcfdff02
Output Block      b9e783b30dd7924ff7bc9b97beaa8740
Plaintext         f69f2445df4f9b17ad2b417be66c3710
Ciphertext        4f78a7f6d29809585a97daec58c6b050
```

F.5.4   CTR-AES192.Decrypt

Key	8e73b0f7da0e6452c810f32b809079e562f8ead2522c6b7b
Init. Counter	f0f1f2f3f4f5f6f7f8f9fafbfcfdfeff

Block #1

Input Block	f0f1f2f3f4f5f6f7f8f9fafbfcfdfeff
Output Block	717d2dc639128334a6167a488ded7921
Ciphertext	1abc932417521ca24f2b0459fe7e6e0b
Plaintext	6bc1bee22e409f96e93d7e117393172a

Block #2

Input Block	f0f1f2f3f4f5f6f7f8f9fafbfcfdff00
Output Block	a72eb3bb14a556734b7bad6ab16100c5
Ciphertext	090339ec0aa6faefd5ccc2c6f4ce8e94
Plaintext	ae2d8a571e03ac9c9eb76fac45af8e51

Block #3

Input Block	f0f1f2f3f4f5f6f7f8f9fafbfcfdff01
Output Block	2efeae2d72b722613446dc7f4c2af918
Ciphertext	1e36b26bd1ebc670d1bd1d665620abf7
Plaintext	30c81c46a35ce411e5fbc1191a0a52ef

Block #4

Input Block	f0f1f2f3f4f5f6f7f8f9fafbfcfdff02
Output Block	b9e783b30dd7924ff7bc9b97beaa8740
Ciphertext	4f78a7f6d29809585a97daec58c6b050
Plaintext	f69f2445df4f9b17ad2b417be66c3710

F.5.5   CTR-AES256.Encrypt

Key	603deb1015ca71be2b73aef0857d7781
	1f352c073b6108d72d9810a30914dff4
Init. Counter	f0f1f2f3f4f5f6f7f8f9fafbfcfdfeff

Block #1

Input Block	f0f1f2f3f4f5f6f7f8f9fafbfcfdfeff
Output Block	0bdf7df1591716335e9a8b15c860c502
Plaintext	6bc1bee22e409f96e93d7e117393172a
Ciphertext	601ec313775789a5b7a7f504bbf3d228

Block #2

Input Block	f0f1f2f3f4f5f6f7f8f9fafbfcfdff00
Output Block	5a6e699d536119065433863c8f657b94
Plaintext	ae2d8a571e03ac9c9eb76fac45af8e51
Ciphertext	f443e3ca4d62b59aca84e990cacaf5c5

Block #3

Input Block	f0f1f2f3f4f5f6f7f8f9fafbfcfdff01
Output Block	1bc12c9c01610d5d0d8bd6a3378eca62
Plaintext	30c81c46a35ce411e5fbc1191a0a52ef
Ciphertext	2b0930daa23de94ce87017ba2d84988d

Block #4

Input Block	f0f1f2f3f4f5f6f7f8f9fafbfcfdff02
Output Block	2956e1c8693536b1bee99c73a31576b6
Plaintext	f69f2445df4f9b17ad2b417be66c3710
Ciphertext	dfc9c58db67aada613c2dd08457941a6

F.5.6   CTR-AES256.Decrypt

Key	603deb1015ca71be2b73aef0857d7781
	1f352c073b6108d72d9810a30914dff4
Init. Counter	f0f1f2f3f4f5f6f7f8f9fafbfcfdfeff

```
Block #1
Input Block      f0f1f2f3f4f5f6f7f8f9fafbfcfdfeff
Output Block     0bdf7df1591716335e9a8b15c860c502
Ciphertext       601ec313775789a5b7a7f504bbf3d228
Plaintext        6bc1bee22e409f96e93d7e117393172a
Block #2
Input Block      f0f1f2f3f4f5f6f7f8f9fafbfcfdff00
Output Block     5a6e699d536119065433863c8f657b94
Ciphertext       f443e3ca4d62b59aca84e990cacaf5c5
Plaintext        ae2d8a571e03ac9c9eb76fac45af8e51
Block #3
Input Block      f0f1f2f3f4f5f6f7f8f9fafbfcfdff01
Output Block     1bc12c9c01610d5d0d8bd6a3378eca62
Ciphertext       2b0930daa23de94ce87017ba2d84988d
Plaintext        30c81c46a35ce411e5fbc1191a0a52ef
Block #4
Input Block      f0f1f2f3f4f5f6f7f8f9fafbfcfdff02
Output Block     2956e1c8693536b1bee99c73a31576b6
Ciphertext       dfc9c58db67aada613c2dd08457941a6
Plaintext        f69f2445df4f9b17ad2b417be66c3710
```

Appendix G: References

[1]   American National Standard for Financial Services X9.52-1998, "Triple Data Encryption Algorithm Modes of Operation." American Bankers Association, Washington, D.C., July 29, 1998.

[2]   FIPS Publication 197, "Advanced Encryption Standard (AES)." U.S. DoC/NIST, November 26, 2001.

[3]   FIPS Publication 46-3, "Data Encryption Standard (DES)." U.S. DoC/NIST, October 25, 1999.

[4]   FIPS Publication 81, "DES Modes of Operation." U.S. DoC/NIST, December 1980.

[5]   A. Menezes, P. van Oorschot, and S. Vanstone, "Handbook of Applied Cryptography." CRC Press, New York, 1997.

www.ingramcontent.com/pod-product-compliance
Lightning Source LLC
Chambersburg PA
CBHW060501060326
40689CB00020B/4604